YIELDING

Prayers for Those in Need of Hope

WILLIAM J. O'MALLEY, SJ

LIGUORI
PUBLICATIONS

One Liguori Drive
Liguori, Missouri 63057-9999
(314) 464-2500

ISBN 0-89243-422-8
Library of Congress Catalog Card Number: 91-76677

Cover and interior design by Pam Hummelsheim
Cover photos by f/STOP PICTURES and Edward Crim

The selections from Scripture used throughout this book have been freely adapted by the author. They are not to be considered or used as official translations.

"A Milkweed" (page 17) by Richard Wilbur. Published by Harcourt Brace Jovanovich, Inc.

"Caliban in the Mines" (page 22) from *Challenge,* copyright © 1914 and renewed 1942 by Louis Untermeyer. Reprinted by permission of Harcourt Brace Jovanovich, Inc.

The hymn on pages 28 and 29 is adapted from "Amazing Grace" by John Newton.

"Conversations in Avila" (page 30) from *Times Three* by Phyllis McGinley. Copyright © 1932-1960 by Phyllis McGinley; copyright © 1938-1942, 1944, 1945, 1958, 1959 by The Curtis Publishing Co. Used by permission of Viking Penguin, a division of Penguin Books USA, Inc.

"The Village Atheist" (page 35) from *Spoon River Anthology* by Edgar Lee Masters, originally published by the Macmillan Company. Permission by Ellen C. Masters.

The Way of Suffering: A Geography of Crisis (pages 40-41 and 140-141) by Jerome Miller. Published by Georgetown University Press.

Acknowledgments continued on page 175.

This book is for
The Rohrers
Marilyn and Bob
Bobby   Tom   Sharon   Trish

God has led us on to know;
The Helmsman lays it down as law
that we must suffer — suffer unto truth.

Even as we sleep,
drop by drop,
remembered pain returns.

And even as we resist,
comes wisdom,
a violent love,
by the awful grace of God.

(Aeschylus,
Agamemnon)

Contents

Introduction

His name was, improbably, Bill Fold, a merchant seaman without family. He was a patient in the Baltimore Marine Hospital, a victim of terminal throat cancer. His larynx had been removed, and he could communicate only in writing. He had also contracted tuberculosis and had to be kept completely isolated. As I sat with him one Saturday, I said, "Bill, it must get terribly lonely." He took his pad and, with a face I can describe only as shining, wrote: "Yes. But isn't it wonderful God trusts me enough to give it to me?"

Bill was one of the few truly great souls I've met in my life, and this book is surely not meant for the likes of him. People of such frightening acceptance and serenity have gone eternities beyond the hope this small volume tries to rouse. Rather, it is intended for those of us (most of us) who are in the lower foothills of the Seven Storey Mountain — perhaps deeper and farther even than that.

Yielding was originally meant for those who face the same challenging gifts of suffering Bill Fold was given — illness and death — with perhaps less exalted souls. But as soon as I happened on the subtitle, I realized that it might serve the needs of those who suffer secondhand as well: the families of those in hospitals and the doctors and nurses who serve them; the bereaved; victims of divorce, whether spouses or children. It reaches out, too, to those whose wounds are just as harrowing but not visible: those lacking self-esteem, plagued with formless anxieties, quagmired in dead-end jobs among unsmiling people, heartsick that life simply won't deliver what they had expected, children whose parents are not like the ones on TV. In the end, this book is intended for all of us, since not one of us is without fears and doubts; all of us are in need of hope.

Who Is in Need of Hope?

Start With Suffering

Suffering is a given. Every philosopher from Buddha to Karl Marx started with suffering. Until we face that painful and inescapable fact of life, we haven't taken even the first step toward discovering what life is about and for. We haven't taken the first step toward wisdom. As Sakini, the little Okinawan interpreter in *Teahouse of the August Moon*, says: "Not easy to learn. Pain make man think. Thought make man wise. Wisdom make life endurable."

The Jews have a delicious curse: "May your life be... interesting," which means, "May it be filled with ogres and giants and dragons that, if you survive, will make a story worth telling." A life without suffering is not a story at all.

Pain is our vocation. Each of our lives is a history of suffering, at least in the broadest sense of giving up something we love very much — or have become accustomed to — in the hope of something better. Birth itself is a traumatic ejection from the closest thing to Nirvana any human will ever know on earth — being fed, warmed, protected, without worries. Then, through no fault of our own, we are thrust suddenly out into the cold and noise, and the first birthday present we get is a slap on the butt! But without that pain, we would die.

Throughout our lives, over and over, we are jerked from our complacent acceptance of the world by the unexpected: weaned and potty trained, shoved out to play with the other nasty kids, betrayed by the all-loving mother at the kindergarten doorway, assaulted by our own suddenly ungovernable and mystifying bodies in adolescence. We become so inured to infuriating interruptions of our well-planned days, to people whose agendas are in direct conflict with our own, to the backbiting of the petty and the sneers of the haughty, that we fail to realize that *is* the way of things. If we were looking for utopia, we landed in the wrong universe.

"How Could a Good God...?"

This book has no answer to that question. Neither does any other. Either there is a good and wise God who has a purpose in pain our parochial minds can't assess — or there are no reasons. According to the latter scenario, we tread water in panic for a while and then we die. And nobody has a reason for it. Life is an absurd joke, and the bitterest irony is that there's no one even to laugh at it, God or meaninglessness.

10

Hence the title: either we yield to God's unknowable purposes or we despair. The whole Book of Job is the story of one man's torment, made all the worse by his unshirkable mind, his relentless need for a reason for punishment so great that if it were in retribution for his sins, it must have been sin so heinous he'd remember it! In the end, however, God doesn't give Job an answer. God *is* the answer. And Job finds that answer not in his calculating wits but in his heart.

We lay hold of our souls only in hell, out in the barren wilderness where there's no escaping God or who we truly are. God comes to us out of the darkness when we most resent joy. It is only when we stop snarling, "I can take care of *myself!*" that we find the truth: that we are not our own. We are God's. And, as Jerome Miller writes, "To be loved…is to be wounded, and no love hurts more, pierces more deeply, than the kind we are completely undeserving to receive."

Often what we call praying is anything but; it is trying to change God's plans rather than trying to come to peace with God's plans. For three full years, I offered Mass solely that God would let my mother die and free her from her torment and me from mine. And God didn't. There was a lesson there that took even more years to penetrate my foolish certitude that God would give me what I wanted if I just prayed hard enough, lived righteously enough, worked unstintingly enough. I did; God didn't.

Prayer As Yielding

Just as Galileo made us realize that the Bible meant something else when it said the sun stood still, God's unwillingness to bend his will to my prayers finally made me realize Jesus must have meant something else when he said every prayer would be answered. It will be. But not with answers, with the Answer.

Pain is not an algebra problem; it's not even a philosophical problem; it's not a "problem" at all. Suffering is a mystery for which we can glean some clues but never a boxed-in answer. As with Job, God does not *give* satisfying answers; God *is* the only satisfying answer.

Praying, then, is a yielding, or it ought to be. Its purpose is not to dominate God but to submit to God, to make some momentary attempt to understand God's ways — not with the calculating intelligence but with the heart. We can't understand our *other* friends with our analytical minds. Then how can we understand our Great Friend with our computer brains? No, the way to understand God, or any friend, is by being-with. That's what the prayers in this book are for: to seduce you into letting go of the reins and letting the great Pegasus take you where he will. If suddenly God clutches at your heart, lay the book aside. It is only a matchmaker.

About the Scripture Readings

The Scripture readings and psalms in *Yielding* are not in any way "official" like the liturgically approved readings in a missal. Rather, they are like those movies that sneak in "as suggested by...," to give at least some nod to the original author. Some of the official psalms can genuinely move my soul, but too many begin with some lovely image like the exiles hanging their harps on the trees in Babylon and end with the suggestion that God bash all Babylonian babies to bits. Sometimes as I was writing, a psalm more or less "took me over" and led me to say things that might puzzle the original psalmist. But when it comes to grappling with God, we're all in this together.

As you move through these prayers, have the courage to surrender. Don't try to control the process or guarantee the outcome. Be humble enough to let God do all the work. Simply yield yourself. You are, after all, the greatest offering you have.

Day One

MORNING

Living God,
Great Alchemist,
you made a universe of nothing.
You made saints of most unlikely souls.
Refine even the dross of my day to gold.
Make me a gift worthy of you.

Presence

Abba, help me know my place.

Grace

Down in the darksome, flinty depths of earth,
where no lordly lion or she-wolf ever prowled,
the lamplit miners pierce the barren rock,
spangled with flashing gold and burning sapphire,
and bring to daylight wonders never known.
But tell me. Where to dig for understanding?
Where can wisdom be refined from all
the darksome, flinty clutter of my days?

Psalm

The powers of darkness mutter, "Certain rumors…,"
but only God knows the depths where wisdom hides.
God alone has traced her path and knows her lair,
for God's eyes pierce the heart of darkness.
It is God alone who wills the weight of wind,
who measures out the waters, unleashes rain,
points the path where thunderclouds may travel.
In the deepest depth, God found where wisdom was,
assessed her worth, refined her, made her his.
"To understand," God says, "return from darkness.
To be wise, you must know your place before your God."
(Job 28:3-12, 23-28)

13

Hymn	Batter my heart, three person'd God; for you As yet but knock, breathe, shine, and seek to mend; That I may rise and stand, o'erthrow me and bend Your force to break, blow, burn and make me new. I, like an usurped town, to another due, Labour to admit you, but oh, to no end; Reason, your viceroy in me, me should defend, But is captived and proved weak or untrue. Yet dearly I love you and would be loved fain, But am betrothed to your enemy: Divorce me, untie or break that knot again, Take me to you, imprison me, for I Except you enthrall me, never shall be free, Nor ever chaste, except you ravish me. <div align="right">(John Donne)</div>
Offering	God, my Friend, this day is yours. I offer you my acceptance of whatever you send — suffering, joy, toil, trouble — ennobled far beyond my means because it comes through the greatest gift you gave me to offer, Jesus, your Son, our Eucharist. I pray not to change your mind, only to understand it, to yield to it. But I do ask you to be with me, especially in.... And I ask your loving watchfulness for my friend.... Help me find you, through the day, beneath all your surprising disguises. Amen.
DAYTIME	
Presence	Living God, for a moment or two inspire me to let go the tiller,

14

to drift awhile on the infinite sea,
to see my problems through your eyes.

Abba, help me see relapse as release.

Grace

God without beginning,
remind me who I am and who you are.
For too long I've smoldered at the unfairness.
I forget, cocooned in this inch or two of life,
how small my pain against the expanse of forever,
tinier than a midge in endless space,
a puff of wind, a momentary shadow, a moth.
Why, then, am I worth your scourge, your wrath?
Like my successes, my sins are petty and inane.
What have I done to merit such attention?
Why single me from all the smiling faceless faces?
Am I more important than I feel?
Could it be what seems your wrath is just your love,
assessed by a fool?

Psalm

(Psalm 39)

When to the sessions of sweet silent thought
I summon up remembrance of things past,
I sigh the lack of many a thing I sought,
And with old woes new wail my dear time's waste.
Then can I drown an eye, unused to flow,
For precious friends hid in death's dateless night,
And weep afresh love's long-since-cancell'd woe,
And moan th' expense of many a vanish'd sight.

Hymn

Then can I grieve at grievances foregone,
And heavily from woe to woe tell o'er
The sad account of fore-bemoaned moan,
Which I new pay as if not paid before.
But if the while I think on Thee, dear Friend,
All losses are restored and sorrows end.

(William Shakespeare)

My mother said [to the wife of a suicide] that she didn't see
how anybody with any faith in God could do such a thing.
[The widow] said oh she was sure he had faith in God, but

Reading

15

he didn't have any faith in people — which is to accuse him of the great asininity....His tragedy was I suppose that he didn't know what to do with his suffering.

(Flannery O'Connor)

Scripture You have forgotten what the Book has always said, haven't you? That we are God's sons and daughters. When a Father reprimands, he doesn't do so lightly, yet he doesn't mean you to be discouraged, either. God gives the heaviest burdens to the ones God loves the best and taxes those who are God's own. Can any Father love, yet let his own just drift, without the challenge to reach further than they'd planned? Without this training, we would be but bastards.

(Hebrews 12:5-8)

Closing God, my Friend,
the day is still one half ahead.
And yet we've made it this far, no?
Which means the two of us
have every chance
to do as well with the rest.
Amen.

EVENING

Presence Living God,
the night comes on,
and I could use a dose of hope.
Help me let go the day
with grace.

Grace Abba, don't let me take myself too seriously.

Psalm As the doe sniffs the air for running waters,
so longs my soul for you, the God of life.
I'm tired of tasting tears all day and night,
while quiet voices whisper, "Where's your God?"
Then with a stab of knowing I remember
how we've walked together side by side before.
Your faithfulness and friendship are forever.
The soul within me melts with joy and hope.

16

Why should a soul so blessed before be downcast?
I sigh no more in sorrow but in release.
I trust and hope in you, my Savior and my God.

(Psalm 42:1-6)

Hymn

"A Milkweed"
Anonymous as cherubs
Over the crib of God,
White seeds are floating
Out of my burst pod.
What power had I
Before I learned to yield?
Shatter me, great wind:
I shall possess the field.

(Richard Wilbur)

Closing

Faithful Friend,
hard as this day has been,
it's not so easy to let it go.
Remind me that today, and tomorrow,
and I
are in your wise hands.
Amen.

Day Two

Presence

Living God,
help me to shred the calendars in my mind,
everything up to today.
Help me surprise everybody with a smile.
Let them guess what's gotten into me.
Five'll getcha ten,
they'll never guess it's you.

Grace

Abba, lift me out of my own way.

Psalm

As a child, Friend, how simple to sing your praise.
Now time and testing have robbed me of a voice
for anything but weary laments and woeful sighs.
I yearn to tell the young your loving kindness,
but my suffering seems to turn my words to lies.
Then let my trust in you — despite the trials you send
— be the word I speak, the song I sing to them.
Let my puzzling joy lure them to learn of you.
My suffering soul is my song of praise to you.
The truth I tell is: to triumph, I must yield.

(Psalm 71)

Hymn

When I consider how my light is spent,
Ere half my days, in this dark world and wide,
And that one talent which is death to hide,
Lodged with me useless, though my soul more bent
To serve therewith my maker, and present
My true account, lest he returning chide,
Doth God exact day-labour, light denied,

I fondly ask; but Patience, to prevent
That murmur, soon replies, God doth not need
Either man's work or his own gifts, who best
Bear his mild yoke, they serve him best, his state
Is kingly: Thousands at his bidding speed,
And post o'er land and ocean without rest:
They also serve who only stand and wait.

(John Milton)

Offering

God, my Friend,
this day is yours.
I offer you my acceptance
of whatever you send —
suffering, joy, toil, trouble —
ennobled far beyond my means
because it comes through the greatest gift
you gave me to offer,
Jesus, your Son, our Eucharist.
I pray not to change your mind,
only to understand it,
to yield to it.
But I do ask you to be with me,
especially in....
And I ask your loving watchfulness
for my friend....
Help me find you, through the day,
beneath all your surprising disguises.
Amen.

DAYTIME

Presence

Living God,
let me be a sheep only with you.
With everyone else I meet,
remind me I'm a shepherd, too.

Grace

Abba, let every gift I give become communion.

Psalm | The Lord is my shepherd. What else is there to want?
He leads my soul into green meadows to rest
by quiet crystal pools where he refreshes me.
And then we rise and make our way on paths
the shepherd's chosen for us. Though some are darksome
I feel no fear when Love strides at my side,
prodding and protecting with crook and staff.
Ahead somewhere, they prepare a gladsome feast
where faces will shine and cups will overflow.
Even mine. Goodness and kindness dog my heels,
urging me on, toward the house of God, where I
will live, beyond all pain, forever and forever.

(Psalm 23)

Hymn | Lord Jesus Christ, I seek to find,
Pray tell me whar He dwells — He dwells.
Oh, you go down in yonder fold
An' search among the sheep — the sheep.

There you will find Him, I am told
He's whar He loves to be — to be.
An' if I find Him, how'll I know
Round any other man — other man?

He has Salvation awn His brow,
He has a wounded han' — wounded han'.
I thank you faw yo' advice —
I'll find Him ef I can — ef I can.

(an unknown black poet)

Reading | The text of the Gospel is concerned only with Christ's presence in the sufferer. Yet it seems as though the spiritual worthiness of him who receives has nothing to do with the matter. It is the benefactor himself, as a bearer of Christ, who causes Christ to enter the famished sufferer with the bread he gives him. The other can consent to receive this presence or not, exactly like the person who goes to communion. If the gift is rightly given, and rightly received, the passing of a morsel of bread from one man to another is something like a real communion.

(Simone Weil)

"Now listen to me. You know that among unbelievers the way to 'prove' yourself is to lord it over people, to make others feel your trivial — and temporary — office bestows some noticeable value on *you*. I do *not* want that to happen among you. No, no!

"If you want to prove your greatness, then you must serve. Test anyone's claims to greatness by how humbly they give their time to all of you. I did not come to be served. I came to serve. The whole reason for my life is to go ransom for you."

(Matthew 20:25-28)

God, my Friend,
as you know, I don't like to be taken advantage of.
I don't like being anyone's dupe, pushover, patsy.
Yet I look at the crucifix.
And I'm forced
to reassess
my priorities.
Amen.

Living God,
something unredeemed in me
tells me I have grounds for complaint
about this day.
Foolish!
Like someone griping
about the accommodations
at a party they had crashed.

Abba, perspective, please?

Save me, God! The deluge overwhelms me.
The surging waters choke me, and my heart
seizes with fear like an iron fist in my chest.
My throat is raw with shouting into the storm,
but the only answer is the lash of wind and waves.

O God, pry open the jaws of this abyss!
Shout! Shout the stormy seas to silence.
Hope of the Hopeless, heed my cry and come.
Help of the Helpless, reach down. Cup me in your hand.
There is no hope or help, except in you.

(Psalm 69)

Hymn

God, we don't like to complain;
We know that the mine is no lark.
But — there's the pools from the rain;
But — there's the cold and the dark.

God, You don't know what it is —
You, in Your well-lighted sky,
Watching the meteors whizz;
Warm, with the sun always by.

God, if You had but the moon
Stuck in Your cap for a lamp,
Even You'd tire of it soon,
Down in the dark and the damp.

Nothing but blackness above,
And nothing that moves but the cars.
God, if You wish for our love,
Fling us a handful of stars!

(Louis Untermeyer)

Closing

Holy Friend,
you're the only one I can honestly talk to,
the only one who sees through the petulance
to the genuine weariness.
I'm so grateful there's Someone
who listens to me,
rather than to what I say.
Amen.

Day Three

Presence

Living God,
all creation submits to you
without thought or hesitation —
except us.
I know that each day
you try to teach me to be docile as they are.
Be patient with me.

Grace

Abba, help me to relent and be at peace.

Psalm

God, your kindness to the earth cascades in rain.
Streams brim, and reeds and lilies drink their fill.
The soil softens, and seedlings spurt to life.
Wherever you move, the womb of earth quickens,
and seed grips down, uncurls, and reaches for
the sun. The grasslands go green and gold with wheat,
hillsides heavy with grapes, pastures flocked.
All the earth shouts and sings for joy!
Life-giving God, my soul is in need of rain.

(Psalm 65)

Hymn

As the marsh hen secretly builds on the watery sod,
Behold I will build me a nest on the greatness of God:
I will fly in the greatness of God
    as the marsh hen flies
In the freedom that fills all the space
    'twixt the marsh and the skies:
By so many roots as the marsh grass sends in the sod
I will heartily lay me a-hold on the greatness of God:
Oh, like to the greatness of God

is the greatness within
The range of the marshes, the liberal marshes of Glynn.

(Sidney Lanier)

Offering

God, my Friend,
this day is yours.
I offer you my acceptance
of whatever you send —
suffering, joy, toil, trouble —
ennobled far beyond my means
because it comes through the greatest gift
you gave me to offer,
Jesus, your Son, our Eucharist.
I pray not to change your mind,
only to understand it,
to yield to it.
But I do ask you to be with me,
especially in....
And I ask your loving watchfulness
for my friend....
Help me find you, through the day,
beneath all your surprising disguises.
Amen.

DAYTIME

Presence

Living God,
my restless, calculating mind
craves answers, neatly wrapped.
Remind me that sometimes
my heart has better eyes.

Grace

Abba, just for a while, let me float.

Psalm

Which of us can know the mind of God?
Who can discern God's will in the nature of things?
Our tests of truth are timid and our plans unsure,
for the fearful flesh has an eye on the cost of truth.
It is hard enough to make sense of life on earth,
to grasp even the truths within our reach.
But things of heaven who can pretend to know?

God, no one can discern your plans for us unless
you send your Spirit to make us truly wise.
It is not with our uppity minds that we will find our way,
but only when you reach out and clasp our hands
and point a path through the darkness into the light.

(Wisdom 9:13-18)

Hymn

They tell me, Lord, that when I seem
To be in speech with you,
Since but one voice is heard, it's all a dream,
One talker aping two.

Sometimes it is, yet not as they
Conceive it. Rather, I
Seek in myself the things I hoped to say,
But lo! my wells are dry.

Then, seeing me empty, you forsake
The listener's role and through
My dumb lips breathe and into utterance wake
The thoughts I never knew.

And thus you neither need reply
Nor can; thus, while we seem
Two talkers, thou art One forever, and I
No dreamer, but thy dream.

(anonymous)

Reading

"I say the gods deal very unrightly with us. For they will
neither (which would be the best of all) go away and leave us
to live our own short days to ourselves, nor will they show
themselves openly and tell us what they would have us do.
For that too would be endurable. But to hint and hover, to
draw near in dreams and oracles, or in a waking vision that
vanishes as soon as seen, to be dead silent when we question
them and then glide back and whisper (words we cannot
understand) in our ears when we most wish to be free of
them, and to show to one what they hide from another; what
is all this but cat-and-mouse play, blindman's buff, and mere
jugglery? Why must holy places be dark places?"

(C.S. Lewis)

Scripture	Wisdom has an aura that never dims. Those who look with loving hearts have no problem seeing her. She has a sense for those who search to understand. They will not find her; she will find them. Watch for her early in the morning, before you have become too busy. You will find her there, sitting at your gate. And during the day she walks about, watching for eyes that are worthy of her, hearts that are ready.
	(Wisdom 6:12-17)
Closing	God, my Friend, quell my restlessness at the slow pace at which you move. Help me to own the truth: that whatever the time you allow me, it is enough. Amen.

EVENING

Presence	Living God, once more I let go of the day. For a while, the world can go its way — as it has for a thousand million years — without my fussing.
Grace	Abba, wrap me in your warm wings.
Psalm	Oh, God, you are my God. I thirst for you like worn-out land, cracked and waterless. Let me feel your presence in my soul, tabernacled there like a tongue of flame. In the night-dark of my bed I lie and think of you, who always have been my light when I let you be. In the shadow of your wings, I sing for joy. They enclose me, warm me, keep me safe from the invader who cannot penetrate my soul.
	(Psalm 63)

That time of year thou mayst in me behold
When yellow leaves, or none, or few, do hang
Upon those boughs which shake against the cold,
Bare ruined choirs, where late the sweet birds sang.
In me thou seest the twilight of such day,
As after sunset fadeth in the west,
Which by and by black night doth take away,
Death's second self, that seals up all in rest.
In me thou seest the glowing of such fire
That on the ashes of his youth doth lie,
As the death-bed whereon it must expire
Consumed with that which it was nourish'd by.
This thou perceivest, which makes thy love more strong,
To love that well which thou must leave ere long.

(William Shakespeare)

Holy Friend,
I keep asking you for peace.
Perhaps you'll help me to understand
that peace is not something I achieve
but only accept.
Amen.

Day Four

Presence Living God,
we have a well-worn cliché
perhaps you've heard:
"Every dark cloud has a...." You have.
Well, as I begin this day,
I'd be grateful if you'd remind me.

Grace Abba, help me to *feel* you near.

Psalm Ah, Holy Friend! Once more you lift me up!
For now, the enemy within withdraws and can
no longer gloat, for you have pulled me back
from the edge of darkness, back into the light!
So long ago, young and smug, I said,
"Hah! Nothing can stop me now!" But then
you hid your face to teach me, and I cringed.
Now, you turn that darkness into dawning!
Mourning leaps to dance! My heart will sing
your praises, Lord. My soul begins to dance.

(Psalm 30)

Hymn Amazing grace! How sweet the sound
That saved a wretch like me!
I once was lost, but now am found,
Was blind, but now I see.

'Twas grace that taught my heart to fear,
And grace my fears relieved;
How precious did that grace appear
The hour I first believed!

28

Through many dangers, toils and snares,
I have already come;
'Tis grace has brought me safe thus far,
And grace will lead me home.

And when we've been there ten thousand years,
Bright shining as the sun,
We'll have no less days to sing God's praise
Than when we first begun.

(John Newton)

Offering

God, my Friend,
this day is yours.
I offer you my acceptance
of whatever you send —
suffering, joy, toil, trouble —
ennobled far beyond my means
because it comes through the greatest gift
you gave me to offer,
Jesus, your Son, our Eucharist.
I pray not to change your mind,
only to understand it,
to yield to it.
But I do ask you to be with me,
especially in....
And I ask your loving watchfulness
for my friend....
Help me find you, through the day,
beneath all your surprising disguises.
Amen.

DAYTIME

Presence

Living God,
more often than I like to admit
I chafe against the way things are,
because I feel
I could arrange them
considerably better than you have.
Can you disabuse me of that?

29

Grace	Abba, show me the way and I'll walk it.
Psalm	Gracious God, you have forgiven my petty sins, and I rest secure in our friendship that they are gone. I know what not to do, but what must I do? Surely you expect much more than shunning sin, prim politeness, clean gray slates. Now, teach me the way to go, the path to you. Like a balky mule, I need a bit and bridle; I can be ornery and cantankerous, as you know. Shatter all my self-serving certitudes. Crack my tiny shell, where I loom so large. Make me see, not with my eyes, but yours. Lord — and I say this with no little trepidation — Take the reins from my hands and into yours.

(Psalm 32)

Hymn	Teresa was God's familiar. She often spoke To Him informally, As if together they shared some heavenly joke. Once, watching stormily Her heart's ambitions wither to odds and ends, With all to start anew, She cried, "If this is the way You treat Your friends, No wonder You have so few!"

There is no perfect record standing by
Of God's reply.

(Phyllis McGinley)

Reading	It is not without reason that we feel a certain uneasy suspicion of that inert phrase, "Christian resignation"; an inner voice reminds us that the Christian God is Love, and that love and resignation can find no common ground to stand on. So much the human creator can tell us, if we like to listen to him. Our confusion on the subject is caused by a dissipation and eclecticism in our associations with the word "love." We connect it too exclusively with the sexual and material passions, whose antipassion is possessiveness, and with indulgent affection, whose antipassion is sentimentality. Concentrated, and freed from its antipassions, love is the Energy of creation:

30

In the juvescence of the year
Came Christ the tiger
— a disturbing thought.

(Dorothy Sayers)

Remember how Yahweh, your God, led you for forty years **Scripture**
in the wilderness, to humble you, to test you so that you
would know your inmost heart as God knows it. God broke
your resistance by making your bellies yearn for food — but
then God gave you manna you had never known or deserved
to show that you cannot live on bread alone but only on the
small cheers and choices and claims God sends you, unex-
pectedly, each day. And you were not abandoned out there,
were you? God was training you as any parent trains a child:
to know the ways of God, to accept them, and to make a life
of them.

(Deuteronomy 8:2-6)

God, my Friend, **Closing**
you know — surely your Son does —
that quite often the things you ask of me
are bitter manna.
Soften my angry heart;
lower my jutting jaw.
I truly would love to love your will
if only I could yield.
Amen.

EVENING

Living God, **Presence**
what makes each day bearable —
sometimes even a joy —
is that at times like this,
when I step aside
to find what's truly important,
I find it: that I'm not alone!

Abba, abide awhile with me. **Grace**

Psalm

Great God,
you are all I need, because you are all I have,
my inheritance, my yokemate, my friend.
In my inmost soul your voice becomes my voice.
You walk at my side, behind, beyond, within.
I am never alone but with and for my God.
My rueful heart exults! My soul sings!
My savaged body soothes and grows serene,
because my God has sought me out and shares
my toil, carries half the burden of my heart,
ennobles my indignities, gives meaning to my pain.
I do not understand the path he chose
but only that he chose it and that he walks with me.

(Psalm 16)

Hymn

God of our fathers, known of old,
Lord of our far-flung battle line,
Beneath whose awful Hand we hold
Dominion over palm and pine —
Lord God of Hosts, be with us yet,
Lest we forget — lest we forget!

The tumult and the shouting dies;
The Captains and the Kings depart:
Still stands Thine ancient sacrifice,
An humble and a contrite heart.
Lord God of Hosts, be with us yet,
Lest we forget — lest we forget!

(Rudyard Kipling)

Closing

Holy Friend,
I lay the day's burden down.
Perhaps someone else
might have handled it better.
But I'm pleased to say
I did the best I could.
Amen.

32

Day Five

Living God,
I place this day in the face of forever,
irretrievably precious for now,
but...no big deal in the end.

Presence

Abba, help me keep a true perspective.

Grace

Fools root their worth in wealth and power and fame,
things that pass like a shadow, a fleeting rumor,
a passing keel that leaves no crease behind.
Birds' wings whip the air in a whirring rush,
yet in a moment there is no sign they were ever there.
The air behind the arrow seals itself again
and goes about its business unimpressed.
And so with us, born astride a grave —
light flashes a moment and all is dark again.
The hope of the godless is dandelion down, borne
on the wind like a passing memory, a one-night guest
who seemed to be important, for a while.
But the wise root their worth in the God who lives forever.
(Wisdom 5:8-17)

Psalm

Not Solomon, for all his wit,
  Nor Samson, though he were so strong,
No king nor person ever yet
  Could 'scape, but death laid him along:
  Wherefore I know that I must die,
  And yet my life amend not I.

Hymn

Though all the East did quake to hear
  Of Alexander's dreadful name,
And all the West did likewise fear
  To hear of Julius Caesar's fame,
  Yet both by death in dust now lie.
  Who then can 'scape, but he must die?

If none can 'scape death's dreadful dart,
  If rich and poor his beck obey,
If strong, if wise, if all do smart,
  Then I to 'scape shall have no way.
  Oh! grant me grace, O God, that I
  My life may mend, sith I must die.

                       (Robert Southwell)

Offering | God, my Friend,
this day is yours.
I offer you my acceptance
of whatever you send —
suffering, joy, toil, trouble —
ennobled far beyond my means
because it comes through the greatest gift
you gave me to offer,
Jesus, your Son, our Eucharist.
I pray not to change your mind,
only to understand it,
to yield to it.
But I do ask you to be with me,
especially in....
And I ask your loving watchfulness
for my friend....
Help me find you, through the day,
beneath all your surprising disguises.
Amen.

DAYTIME

Presence | Living God,
I've already had my minor setbacks today
and, knowing you,
I probably haven't seen the last of them.

34

Help me to see each setback
as a call forward
to more than I thought I could do.

Abba, blow on the embers of my hope. **Grace**

Psalm
Do not disdain the discipline of the Lord or lose heart and
grow discouraged when you are tried. God trains the ones he
loves and calls his own. When you endure with courage, God
loves you most, for suffering conquered is the only way to
grow. Could a parent love and never say, "Try again"? Those
never tried are not God's own but bastards.

(Hebrews 12:5-9)

Hymn
Ye young debaters over the doctrine
Of the soul's immortality.
I who lie here was the village atheist,
Talkative, contentious, versed in the arguments
Of the infidels.
But through a long sickness
Coughing myself to death
I read the Upanishads and the poetry of Jesus.
And they lighted a torch of hope and intuition
And desire which the Shadow,
Leading me through the caverns of darkness,
Could not extinguish.
Listen to me, ye who live in the senses
And think through the senses only:
Immortality is not a gift,
Immortality is an achievement:
And only those who strive mightily
Shall possess it.

(Edgar Lee Masters)

Reading
We have remarked that one reason offered for being a progressive is that things naturally tend to grow better. But the
only real reason for being a progressive is that things naturally tend to grow worse. The corruption in things is not only
the best argument for being progressive; it is also the only
argument against being conservative. The conservative
theory would really be quite sweeping and unanswerable if

it were not for this one fact. But all conservatism is based upon the idea that if you leave things alone you leave them as they are. But you do not. If you leave a thing alone you leave it to a torrent of change. If you leave a white post alone it will soon be a black post. If you particularly want it to be white you must be always painting it again; that is, you must be always having a revolution. Briefly, if you want the old white post you must have a new white post.

(G.K. Chesterton)

Scripture Think of God's mercy, my friends, and worship God in a way worthy of men and women with minds. Offer each day as a living sacrifice, offering it in service to others and to God. Now that is true worship. Don't gear your choices to the self-absorbed "lifestyle" of those around you and the theory "Everyone does it!" Think! Let God transform you inwardly by a complete renewal of your mind. That is the only way you will discover the will of God — what God really wants, what will make you truly whole.

(Romans 12:1-2)

Closing God, my Friend,
I truly want to be a self,
a never-before-or-again me.
But all the voices around me —
my family, my friends, my clients, the boss, the ads —
sneer and try to snare me to be
just like everyone else.
Help me to stake an inviolable claim
on my own soul.
Amen.

EVENING

Presence Living God,
what can I offer in return
for this chance to be alive?
I offer what I've made of this day.
I hope — I know — it will do.

Grace Abba, even as the day slips away, let me shine!

36

"Comfort my people!" says our God. "Console them!
Tell them that they have suffered long enough.
Heal their hearts. Their sins are wiped from my mind.
Prepare in their barren hearts a highway for me.
Every valley shall exult, every hill bow low,
and the glory of God shall be revealed in us.
Go up to the high mountain, my friend, and shout:
'Here comes your God! A shepherd feeding his flock,
gathering his lambs to his chest in a hug of joy!' "

(Isaiah 40:1-11)

Done foun' my los' sheep,
Done foun' my los' sheep,
Done foun' my los' sheep,
Hallelujah!
Done foun' my los' sheep.

My Lord had a hundred sheep,
One o' dem did go astray.
That lef' Him ninety-nine.
Go to the wilderness, seek an' fin'.
Ef you fin' him, bring him back,
Cross de shoulders, cross de back;
Tell de neighbors all aroun',
Dat los' sheep has done been foun'.

In dat Resurrection Day
Sinner can find no hidin' place.
Go to the mountain, de mountain move!
Run to the hill, de hill run, too!
Sinner man treadin' on tremblin' groun',
Po' los' sheep ain't nebber been foun'.
Sinner why don' you stop an' pray?
Den you'd hear the Shepherd say:
Done foun' my los' sheep,
Done foun' my los' sheep,
Done foun' my los' sheep!

(an unknown black poet)

Holy Friend, it's good to be home.
Amen.

Day Six

Presence | Living God,
your Spirit once went to a hill-country girl
and asked her permission
to conceive your Son within her.
Today I would like to conceive your Son
in me.

Grace | Abba, let my life bring forth life.

Psalm | My joyful soul gives witness to the greatness of God,
and my spirit sings for joy over God, my savior!
His eyes have looked right through my lowliness.
Ah! From now, all people will know how he's gifted me.
The God whose name is holy has entered my home!
His mercy is forever for those who bow to his will.
His mighty arm scatters the proud and their plans,
pulls down princes and puts the poor in their place,
feeds the needy and sends the rich, empty, away.
(Luke 1:46-53)

Hymn | At morn, at noon, at twilight dim,
Maria, thou hast heard my hymn!
In joy and woe, in good and ill,
Mother of God, be with me still!
When the hours flew brightly by,
And not a cloud obscured the sky,
My soul, lest it should truant be,
Thy grace did guide to thine and thee;
Now, when the storms of fate o'ercast
Darkly my present and my past,

38

Let my future radiant shine
With sweet hopes of thee and thine.

(Edgar Allan Poe)

God, my Friend,
this day is yours.
I offer you my acceptance
of whatever you send —
suffering, joy, toil, trouble —
ennobled far beyond my means
because it comes through the greatest gift
you gave me to offer,
Jesus, your Son, our Eucharist.
I pray not to change your mind,
only to understand it,
to yield to it.
But I do ask you to be with me,
especially in....
And I ask your loving watchfulness
for my friend....
Help me find you, through the day,
beneath all your surprising disguises.
Amen.

Offering

DAYTIME

Living God,
for these few moments
pull off the road with me
to remind me you are God;
it's not all up to me.

Presence

Abba, rescue me from fear.

Grace

I thrashed in quicksand, and the Lord bent down to me,
pulled me from the mire, and set my feet on rock.
My panicked heart subsides, and I can breathe!
Steady my steps, O Lord. I am wobbly as a child,
reborn from the womb of pain, learning again,
this time in a world far bleaker than before.
Tumbling into mire, the rescue, the bleak new world —

Psalm

39

I make no pretense to understand, except
that in the scroll of the Book I'm told I'm to obey.
You are the God who called me forth from nothingness.
Thus, every day is a gift I don't deserve.
I did nothing to merit these days of pain — and yet
Neither did I merit the days of joy and peace,
the heedless laughter, rejoicing, those I love.
Help me not to forget just who you are.
And who I am.

(Psalm 40)

Hymn   But country folks who live beneath
　　　The shadow of the steeple;
　　The parson and the parson's wife,
　　　And mostly married people;

　　Youths green and happy in first love,
　　　So thankful for illusion;
　　And men caught out in what the world
　　　Calls guilt, in first confusion;

　　And almost everyone when age,
　　　Disease, or sorrows strike him,
　　Inclines to think there is a God,
　　　Or something very like him.

(Arthur Hugh Clough)

Reading   It is not that we find God and then realize he created us from
nothing. Rather, it is only in finding our own nothingness and
embracing it that we realize God exists. For only an encounter
with nothingness takes us far enough outside our world for
us to realize there is a giver of being who does not belong to
it. One finds God by dying. And what dies last and most
reluctantly is our longing to be important, to be beings in our
own right, our not wanting to shrink, in mortifying embarrassment, into our own nothingness. For in suffering that
embarrassment, in acknowledging one's own nothingness,
one discovers for the first time one's true and utter unworthiness. And only someone suffering, in all its mortifying
anguish, that sense of unworthiness, of not deserving to exist,
is in a position to know what it means to be loved into being

40

by God. For it is precisely in our nothingness, and nowhere else, that God loves us. To be loved, we said, is to be wounded, and no love hurts more, pierces more deeply than the kind we are completely undeserving to receive.

(Jerome Miller)

Scripture

In your minds you must be just as Jesus was. He was, from forever, God, and yet he did not regard equality with God as something to be grappled to himself. Instead, he emptied himself in order to become a slave, a human being as we are. Humbler yet, he bowed himself before death — and a slave's death on a cross at that! For that, God raised him up again and gave him back the name which is beyond all other names, so that every creature in heaven and on the earth and under the earth should bend the knee and cry, "Jesus is Lord!"

(Philippians 2:5-11)

Closing

God, my Friend,
it is a terrifying request
to ask you to break me
even more than I have been broken.
But if that is truly the only way,
keep a tight hold on my hand.
Amen.

EVENING

Presence

Living God,
the day winds down,
and, to be honest, I do too.
I tell you not to keep you abreast of the latest news
but more, I suppose, to tell myself,
knowing Someone who cares
is interested,
if not in my news,
in me.

Grace

Abba, let me take all as gift and not for granted.

Psalm | Praise God, you heavenly heights! Praise God!
Fevered sun and silver moon, praise God!
Glittering stars and frigid space, praise God!
Curmudgeon thunder and rhinestone rain, praise God!

Let all that have God's life in them sing praise!
Sargasso weed and black-eyed Susan, cactus,
Queen Anne's lace, Kentucky grass, and limes,
plump pumpkins, peaches, pears — praise God!

Let all that have God's urge to roam sing praise!
Elegant dolphin, lean-shanked hare and hound,
trumpeter, tusker, wombat, wallaby, worm,
kingfisher, kangaroo, kinkaju — praise God!

Let all who have God's deathless soul sing praise!
Pope and prince, president, pasha, peer,
Faust and housewife, lifeguard, barkeep, sweep,
squatter, vagrant, sot and serf — praise God!

Praise God! Praise God!
  Let all God's children praise God!

(Psalm 148)

Hymn | I walked beside the deep, one night of stars;
No cloud above, no sail upon the sea.
All nature seemed to question waves and sky
Of their dread majesty and mystery.

And the great breakers bowed their haughty crests,
And thundered forth, with voice of full accord
The diapason of their ceaseless hymn
Of "Holy, holy, holy to the Lord!"

The starry legions cast their crowns of fire
Before the feet of God, and made reply,
In swelling anthems jubilant and strong,
"It is the Lord! It is the Lord Most High!"

(Victor Hugo)

Holy Friend,
amidst the chorus of all those stars
and thundering waves,
I offer the small song
of my today.
Amen.

Day Seven

Presence | Living God,
you're consistently generous
at giving me mornings,
one more chance again.
Help me be worthy
of your kindness.

Grace | Abba, give me a confident heart.

Psalm | God's storehouse opens and clouds fly out like birds.
He wrings them to rain and shivers them to hail.
His voice flashes fire and thunders through the hills.
And his morning mist heals everything in time.
No words can grasp our God, the all in all.
Since we cannot fathom him, then let us praise,
for greater is God than all the works of his hands,
and only a few of his works have we even seen!
Awesome is his majesty; wonderful is his power.
As your strength wanes, praise him all the more!
God shares his power with all who dare to hope.

(Sirach 43:14-16, 28-35)

Hymn | Let all the world in ev'ry corner sing
My God and King.
The heav'ns are not too high,
His praise may thither fly;
The earth is not too low,
His praises there may grow.
Let all the world in ev'ry corner sing
My God and King.

44

The Church with psalms must shout,
No door can keep them out:
But above all, the heart
Must bear the longest part.

(George Herbert)

Offering

God, my Friend,
this day is yours.
I offer you my acceptance
of whatever you send —
suffering, joy, toil, trouble —
ennobled far beyond my means
because it comes through the greatest gift
you gave me to offer,
Jesus, your Son, our Eucharist.
I pray not to change your mind,
only to understand it,
to yield to it.
But I do ask you to be with me,
especially in....
And I ask your loving watchfulness
for my friend....
Help me find you, through the day,
beneath all your surprising disguises.
Amen.

DAYTIME

Presence

Living God,
you've shown yourself adept
at bringing cosmos out of chaos,
sight with mud and spittle,
life from death.
At the moment,
I have some pretty inauspicious material
from which to create a life.
I would appreciate your advice.

Abba, show me ways to turn my worries into wisdom.

Grace

Psalm	"Yes, confusion and weeping are the way of things. While others seem to go their way serene, you will have this inner burden to bear. Patience, friends! Your sorrow will turn to joy. When a woman is gripped with knowing her time is come, her mind floods with fear of the agony ahead. But she walks through the dark valley with purpose, for she knows that someone priceless awaits her there. When that new life is finally laid in her arms, the memory of her terror and torment melts away, for the soul that waited within her womb is here! The feel of that flesh makes the pain seem nothing. So with you; your suffering is gestating joy!"

(John 16:20-23)

Hymn	Christ, carpenter: "I make the wonderful carven beams Of cedar and of oak To build King Solomon's house of dreams With many a hammer-stroke, And the gilded, wide-winged cherubims.
	"I have no thought in my heart but this: How bright will be my bower When all is finished; My joy it is To see each perfect flower Curve itself up to the tool's harsh kiss.
	"How shall I end the thing I planned? Such knots are in the wood! With quivering limbs I stoop and stand, My sweat runs down like blood — I have driven the chisel through My hand."

(Dorothy Sayers)

Reading	In the morality of my station and duties [i.e. of the moral code] the station presents us with the duty, and we say "Yes" or "No." "I will" or "I will not." We choose between obeying or disobeying a given command. In the morality of challenge or grace [in contrast] the situation says, "Here is a mess, a crying evil, a need! What can you do about it?" We are asked

46

not to say "Yes" or "No" or "I will" or "I will not," but to be inventive, to create, to discover something new. The difference between ordinary people and saints is not that saints fulfill the plain duties which ordinary men neglect. The things saints do have not usually occurred to ordinary people at all…"Gracious" conduct is somehow like the work of an artist. It needs imagination and spontaneity. It is not a choice between presented alternatives but the creation of something new.

(A.D. Lindsay)

I saw a new heaven and a new earth, for the first heaven and earth had been scoured away. And I heard a loud voice from the throne cry: "You see this new city? From now on, here, God will dwell among you, for his name is Emmanuel: God with us. He will wipe away every tear, and there will be no more mourning or sadness or death. The world of the past is gone. Then the One sitting on the throne declared: "Behold! I make all things new!"	Scripture

(Revelation 21:1-5)

God, my Friend,	Closing

God, my Friend,
perhaps it's time
for a little housecleaning of the soul.
Help me to determine
what I'm addicted to that is dragging me down,
what I've neglected to take out and shine,
what I detest that is a call to grow.
Amen.

EVENING

Living God,	Presence

Living God,
too long they've trained me
to picture you as my judge.
It will probably take a bit of time
to convince me that, instead,
you are my defender.

Abba, help me to appreciate my honest worth.

Grace

47

Psalm | With God on our side, who can be against us?
God did not spare the Son, but gave him up, for us.
After such a gift, would God deny a lesser one?
Could anyone condemn those whom God has acquitted?
Could Christ Jesus — who died and rose only for us?
No, no! He does not accuse; he pleads our cause.
Therefore nothing — nothing whatever in heaven or earth
— can come between us and the love of Christ, our Lord.
Oh, yes, troubles and worries will come in battalions.
Stripped to the soul, we will be mauled and harried.
Scripture promised: "For God, we are daily doomed
and reckoned no better than dumb sheep for slaughter."
But I am dead certain of this: neither life nor death,
no angel or prince, nothing now or yet to come,
no power or height or depth or any created thing
can come between us and the relentless love of God
made visible once for all in Christ Jesus our Lord.

(Romans 8:31-39)

Hymn | Then the blest paths we'll travel
Strewed with rubies thick as gravel,
Ceilings of diamonds, sapphire floors,
High wall of coral, and pearly bowers.
From thence to Heaven's bribeless hall,
Where no corrupted voices brawl;
No conscience molten into gold,
No forged accuser bought or sold,
No cause deferred, no vain-spent journey,
For there Christ is the King's Attorney;
Who pleads for all without degrees,
And He hath angels, but no fees;
And when the grand twelve-million jury
Of our sins, with direful fury,
'Gainst our souls black verdicts give,
Christ pleads His death and then we live.

(Sir Walter Raleigh)

Holy Friend,
I leave a great deal still undone,
but that's what you make tomorrows for.
"Sufficient today are the evils thereof"
but sufficient as well the successes.
For both of which
I thank you.
Amen.

Day Eight

Presence | Living God,
if you would be so kind,
while I crank up my body,
would you please crank up my heart?

Grace | Abba, ignite my willingness to laugh.

Psalm | Do not slip into the swamp of brooding sadness.
A glad heart is the pulse of human life,
and your joy is a gift to everyone — and you.
Surprise yourself to distract you from your cares;
have the courage to send resentment on its way,
for more than a few have worried themselves to death,
and sulkiness hurts no tormentor but yourself.
Jealousy, anger, and worry shrivel your days
and lace the finest meal with bitterness,
while a cheerful heart makes mere bread a joy.

(Sirach 30:21-25)

Hymn | While we slumber and sleep
The sun leaps up from the deep
— Daylight born at a leap! —
Rapid, dominant, free,
Athirst to bathe in the uttermost sea.

While we linger at play
— If the year would stand at May! —
Winds are up and away
Over land, over sea,
To their goal wherever their goal may be.

It is time to arise,
To race for the promised prize,
— The Sun flies, the Wind flies —
We are strong, we are free,
And home lies beyond the stars and the sea.

(Christina Georgina Rossetti)

God, my Friend,
this day is yours.
I offer you my acceptance
of whatever you send —
suffering, joy, toil, trouble —
ennobled far beyond my means
because it comes through the greatest gift
you gave me to offer,
Jesus, your Son, our Eucharist.
I pray not to change your mind,
only to understand it,
to yield to it.
But I do ask you to be with me,
especially in....
And I ask your loving watchfulness
for my friend....
Help me find you, through the day,
beneath all your surprising disguises.
Amen.

Living God,
you made me free not to love,
to settle for the tested, trusted few,
to impoverish my soul.
For my own good, then,
steer a few sadder souls than mine
my way.

Abba, don't let me be complacent, preaching love.

If you refuse to love, your life is worse than death.
If you hate anyone, then you are his murderer —

51

and murderers, as you know, have only death in them.
This taught us love: that Christ gave his life to us,
and we ought to give our lives to one another.
If a rich man tells a pauper, "Have a nice day!"
how could the love of God be living in him?
My friends, our love cannot be merely talk.
Love is an active verb and not a noun.
Only by this are we certain we're children of truth
and able with peaceful conscience to face our God.
No matter what accusations our consciences raise,
God is greater than conscience and knows the truth.

(1 John 3:15-20)

Hymn

In this world those who love me
try by all means
to keep me tied to them.

Your love is greater than theirs
and still you left me free.

Afraid that I would forget them
they don't dare to leave me alone.

But days pass by
one after the other
and You never let yourself be seen.

I do not call upon you in my prayer
I do not have you in my heart,
and yet your love for me
still awaits my love.

(Rabindranath Tagore)

Reading

When he told me that he had many friends, could easily make
news ones and have a high old time with them, it struck me
like a blow which had been very carefully aimed. A question
had become meaningless.

I understood only much later, understood that his words
had hurt so because my love had still a long way to go before
it would mature into — love.

(Dag Hammarskjöld)

52

All I want is you, joyful, always happy in the Lord! I repeat: I just want your joy. Make your kindness obvious. The Lord is at your shoulder. Put aside all your anxieties, but if there is something you need, pray for it, asking God in gratitude for all he's already given, and at the very least you will know that peace of God which is beyond any human capacity to encompass it. Finally, fill your minds with everything true, everything noble, everything pure and good, everything lovely and honorable, everything virtuous and worthy of praise. Live your life like that, and God's peace will find you.
(Philippians 4:4-9)

Scripture

God, my Friend,
remind me that love is not a feeling
but an act of the will,
that love takes over when the feelings fail,
when the beloved is no longer even likable.
Amen.

Closing

EVENING

Living God,
we come again to the eye
between the hurricanes,
when the two of us can pull back
and ponder what's truly important.

Presence

Abba, help me be honest.

Grace

Choose a map only when you know where you're going.
Hold consistent convictions but be open to learn.
Be eager to listen but slow to give your reply.
When you know nothing, put your hand over your mouth
or you will end up tripping over your own tongue.
Do not take refuge in tangles of tiny lies
or you will end up choked in your own deceits.
Beware of small offenses as you would of great,
for an avalanche begins with a single stone.
(Sirach 5:11-17)

Psalm

53

Hymn

Happy those early dayes! when I
Shin'd in my angell-infancy.
Before I understood this place
Appointed for my second race,
Or taught my soul to fancy aught
But a white, celestiall thought.
When yet I had not walk'd above
A mile or two from my first love,
And, looking back (at that short space),
Could see a glimpse of his bright face;
When on some gilded cloud or flow're
My gazing soul would dwell an houre,
And in those weaker glories spy
Some shadows of eternity.

(Henry Vaughan)

Closing

Holy Friend,
we come to the end
of what has not been a perfect day.
But as Mercutio quipped, " 'T'will do."
And my eternal thanks for it.
Amen.

Day Nine

Living God,
I know you'll betray my expectations of today.
If only I had more willingness to play
rather than to control.

Presence

Abba, let me be willing to be led.

Grace

Idler, take a lesson from the ant.
Her heart is more attuned to God than yours.
She has no foreman, no taskmaster, no boss,
yet all summer she toils from dawn till after dusk,
storing against the days she cannot toil.
She yields to the task God sets for her today.
How long will you sit there dribbling time away,
moping and wishing your life were otherwise?
You are imprisoned in your dreams of might-have-been,
self-condemned to circumvent the truth.
Live with what you have and are. Or die.

(Proverbs 6:6-11)

Psalm

Little Lamb, who made thee?
Dost thou know who made thee?
Gave the life and bade thee feed,
By the stream and o'er the mead;
Gave thee clothing of delight,
Softest clothing, wooly, bright,
Gave thee such a tender voice,
Making all the vales rejoice?
Little Lamb, who made thee?
Dost thou know who made thee?

Hymn

55

Little Lamb, I'll tell thee;
Little Lamb, I'll tell thee;
He is called by thy name,
For He calls Himself a Lamb.
He is meek and He is mild;
He became a little child.
I a child, and thou a Lamb,
We are called by His name.
Little Lamb, God bless thee!
Little Lamb, God bless thee!

(William Blake)

Offering | God, my Friend,
this day is yours.
I offer you my acceptance
of whatever you send —
suffering, joy, toil, trouble —
ennobled far beyond my means
because it comes through the greatest gift
you gave me to offer,
Jesus, your Son, our Eucharist.
I pray not to change your mind,
only to understand it,
to yield to it.
But I do ask you to be with me,
especially in....
And I ask your loving watchfulness
for my friend....
Help me find you, through the day,
beneath all your surprising disguises.
Amen.

DAYTIME

Presence | Living God,
"they" never tire of telling me what's important.
Oh, sweet Christ, *free* me of what "they" think!
Free me of the ephemerals and the fake.
Free me from envying the truly unenviable.

Grace | Abba, they won't play three-card monte with my soul.

56

The staples of life are water, food, and clothes,
and a small place on which you can close the door.
But better life in a hovel of one's own
than banquets in the halls of condescending strangers.
It is a bitter life to beg from house to house,
eating the bread of scorn with eyes cast down,
charity sweet to give and bitter to receive.
A grudging gift is not a gift at all
but rather a bribe to get you out of sight
as if one had to beg for dignity.
Be it little or much, be content with what you have,
and pay no heed to those who sneer at your lot.

(Sirach 29:21-28)

These I have loved.
White plates and cups, clean-gleaming,
Ringed with blue lines; and feathery, faery dust;
Wet roofs, beneath the lamplight; the strong crust
Of friendly bread; and many-tasting food;
Rainbows; and the blue bitter smoke of wood;
And radiant raindrops couching in cool flowers;
And flowers themselves, that sway through sunny hours,
Dreaming of moths that drink them under the moon;
Then, the cool kindliness of sheets, that soon
Smooth away trouble; and the rough male kiss
Of blankets; grainy wood; live hair that is
Shining and free; blue-massing clouds; the keen
Unpassioned beauty of a great machine;
The benison of hot water; furs to touch;
The good smell of old clothes; and other such —
The comfortable smell of friendly fingers,
Hair's fragrance, and the musty reek that lingers
About dead leaves and last year's ferns....

(Rupert Brooke)

The ineffable inhabits the magnificent and the common, the
grandiose and the tiny facts of reality alike. Some people
sense this quality at distant intervals in extraordinary events;
others sense it in the ordinary events, in every fold, in every
nook; day after day, hour after hour. To them things are bereft
of triteness....Slight and simple as things may be — a piece

of paper, a morsel of bread, a word, a sigh — they hide a never-ending secret: a glimpse of God? kinship with the spirit of being? an eternal flash of a will?

(Abraham Heschel)

Scripture | I have learned to manage with whatever I have. I certainly know what it's like to be poor, and I've had my taste of good living, too. Once you've been through both, you slowly begin to know what's really important. Then, you're ready for anything, anywhere — full belly or empty, fat purse or flat purse. There is nothing I can't take, as long as God lets me know I'm not alone.

(Philippians 4:11-14)

Closing | God, my Friend,
there's a romance in the ordinary
I don't often allow myself to see.
I'm so easily seduced by surfaces.
Do some work on my eyes,
my yearnings,
my weakness.
Amen.

EVENING

Presence | Living God,
I'm not into thunder thoughts
at the end of the day.
You found much to your liking, I hear,
from Abraham and Sarah, barren as brick,
from Moses, the stammerer, Gideon, who cringed,
the first pope, who denied you three times.
You have called me to comfortable company.

Grace | Abba, I am rickety, but let me make a stand.

Psalm | Shame without change is mere displeasure with oneself,
but shame that harrows the heart deserves respect.
Pettiness makes your heart like the pit of a peach,
and cowardice gives its victims a taste for dust.
Speak when there is need, and share your hard-won truth

so the young may share your wisdom without your scars.
Do not strive against the river's flow
or against the painful barbs of unpleasant truths.
Do not merely blush for ignorance or sin
but confess them open-heartedly and change.
Do not grovel to a bully or entertain a fool
or save your smiles for men of pedigree.
Fight to the death for truth with God at your side.
Make no proud boasts, then slink shamefaced away.
Be not a lion at home and a mouse in the marketplace.
Let not your hands be spread when it's time to receive
but clenched like iron knots when it's time to give.

(Sirach 4:20-31)

Hymn

If thou shouldst never see my face again,
Pray for my soul. More things are wrought by prayer
Than this world dreams of. Wherefore, let thy voice
Rise like a fountain for me night and day.
For what are men better than sheep or goats
That nourish a blind life within the brain,
If, knowing God, they lift not hands of prayer
Both for themselves and those who call them friend?
For so the whole round earth is every way
Bound by gold chains about the feet of God.

(Alfred, Lord Tennyson)

Closing

Holy Friend,
easy enough, at the end of the day,
to say what I should have done.
But I did what I did
with an honest heart.
And I'm not ashamed.
Amen.

Day Ten

Presence | Living God,
the poet said,
"Hope is a thing with feathers."
She was right; hope is a skittery thing.
I would beg you, out of kindness,
to let hope alight once more,
bright-winged on my shoulder.

Grace | Abba, save me from the jails of my own building.

Psalm | Lord, in your presence, no living soul is just.
If you call me to judgment, my case is open and shut.
I am dungeoned here, and my heart is drained of hope.
When dawn seeps into my cell, remind me, Lord.
Remind me of the days when I knew we were friends,
when I took your loving-kindness as a given.
I know that there were times I hid from you.
But, Lord, you bear no grudges. Don't hide from me!
My hands grope the gritty walls for a gate.
You are the gateway, God. Where have you gone?
God, in your goodness rescue me as you promised.
But if it is your will that I remain, then teach me.
If you cannot give me freedom, give me patience.

(Psalm 143)

Hymn | I mean to lift up a standard faw my King,
All ovuh this world I mean to sing.

When Daniel was called by wicked men,
They cast po' Daniel in de liyun's den;

Daniel went down feelin' no fear,
Because he knew his God was near.

When Daniel found out a writin' was signed,
He went to his room in his own set time;
He fell on his knees an' begin to pray,
An' in this sperit I heard him say:
"I mean to lift up a standard faw my King,
All ovuh this world I mean to sing!"

When the King had signed that wicked decree,
Daniel was found down on his knees;
"I'm goin' to pray three times a day,
An' look to Jesus to open the way."

The King was in trouble all night long,
He felt that he treated po' Daniel wrong;
He went down early next mawnin' to see,
"King, the God I serve has delivud me."

(an unknown black poet)

God, my Friend,
this day is yours.
I offer you my acceptance
of whatever you send —
suffering, joy, toil, trouble —
ennobled far beyond my means
because it comes through the greatest gift
you gave me to offer,
Jesus, your Son, our Eucharist.
I pray not to change your mind,
only to understand it,
to yield to it.
But I do ask you to be with me,
especially in....
And I ask your loving watchfulness
for my friend....
Help me find you, through the day,
beneath all your surprising disguises.
Amen.

Offering

61

Presence | Living God,
on the surface I'm quite sophisticated,
quick with a quip,
always on the *qui vive*.
When I begin posturing,
give me a nudge.

Grace | Abba, today, let me not be a burden, even to me.

Psalm | God, I am tangled in a net of confusion and doubts,
about myself, my friends, today, tomorrow — you.
My eyes are weary of weeping; my bones wither;
I am sick of feeling sorry for myself,
and those who know me are sickened by it, too.
I'm an unwelcome burden to them and to myself.
Heal me! Heal me, even despite myself!
Make me remember that you have made me to live.
Help me to put myself aside and see
that what seems the wrath of God
is the love of God assessed by a fool.

(Psalm 31)

Hymn | An agnostic artist speaks to Our Lady:
Help me to know! not with my mocking art —
  With you, who knew yourself unbound by laws;
Gave God your strength, your Life, your sight, your heart,
  And took from Him the Thought that Is — the Cause.

Help me to feel! not with my insect sense —
  With yours that felt all life alive in you;
Infinite heart beating at your expense;
  Infinite passion breathing the breath you drew!

Help me to bear! not my own baby load,
  But yours; who bore the failure of the light,
The strength, the knowledge and the thought of God,
  The futile folly of the infinite.

(Henry Adams)

I think there is no suffering greater than what is caused by |
the doubts of those who want to believe. I know what torment
this is but I can only see it, in myself anyway, as the process
by which faith is deepened. A faith that just accepts is a child's
faith and all right for children, but eventually you have to
grow religiously as every other way, though some never do.

What people don't realize is how much religion costs. They
think faith is a big electric blanket, when of course it is the
cross. It is much harder to believe than not to believe. If you
feel you can't believe, you must at least do this: keep an open
mind. Keep it open toward faith, keep wanting it, keep asking
for it, and leave the rest to God.

(Flannery O'Connor)

They brought a boy to him, racked with convulsions, and he
lay writhing there, foaming at the mouth. Jesus asked the
boy's father, "How long has this been going on?" And the
father replied, "From childhood. Sometimes it throws him
into the fire. But if you can help us, sir, have pity on us." Jesus
cocked an eye at him. " 'If you can?' " he smiled. "Isn't
anything possible to those who have faith?" And the boy's
father cried out, "I *do* have faith! Oh, please! Help the little
faith I have!"

(Mark 9:20-24)

God, my Friend,
I believe.
Help my unbelief.
Amen.

Living God,
humility is truth they tell me.
Then why do I, falsely, pick over my faults
almost with an abject pride,
happy to be no better
than any other of your enemies?

Grace	Abba, let me not be afraid to be honestly proud.
Psalm	Refuse not a kindness to anyone who begs for it.

Grace Abba, let me not be afraid to be honestly proud.

Psalm Refuse not a kindness to anyone who begs for it.
Do not say to your neighbor, "It's inconvenient now.
Come back tomorrow," when you could give today.
Don't plot against your neighbor, who trusts in you.
Don't envy the arrogant, who only seem to prosper,
for the Lord sees beyond the surface to the soul
and sorts arrogance from pride like weeds from wheat.
The land is for those with open hands and hearts.
In the end, God will mock those who mock
and open his arms to those with open arms.

(Proverbs 3:27-35)

Hymn Abou Ben Adhem (may his tribe increase!)
Awoke one night from a deep dream of peace
And saw, within the moonlight in his room,
Making it rich, and like a lily in bloom,

An angel writing in a book of gold:
Exceeding peace had made Ben Adhem bold,
And to the presence in the room he said,
"What writest thou?" — The vision raised its head.
And with a look made of all sweet accord,
Answered, "The names of those that love the Lord."

And is mine one?" said Abou. "Nay, not so,"
Replied the angel. Abou spoke more low,
But cheerly still; and said, "I pray thee then,
Write me as one that loves his fellow men."

The angel wrote, and vanished. The next night
It came again with a great wakening light
And showed the names whom love of God had blessed,
And lo! Ben Adhem's name led all the rest.

(Leigh Hunt)

Holy Friend,
with humble pride
I let go of this day.
If there were anything I had done
seriously to upset our friendship,
surely I would know and apologize.
You know — and I know — I tried.
Amen.

Day Eleven

Presence | Living God,
I'm like a yearling chafing at the gate.
I want to get out there and make things happen!
Patience is a virtue in which I need
some remedial education.

Grace | Abba, help me make a truce with time.

Psalm | Am I so deep into the depths you cannot hear,
a place your infinite compassion cannot plumb?
I know if you kept a record of our sins,
the best of us could not emerge unscathed.
Forgetful God, when you amnesty my sins,
forget not me. I wait for you as eagerly
as watchmen wait for dawn. I wait. I wait.
I wait in trust. Fading. But I wait.

(Psalm 130)

Hymn | I am waiting for no one:
but he must come,
he will come, if I hold out
blossoming unseen,
he will come suddenly,
when I am least aware:
he will come almost as forgiveness
of so much death that he causes,
he will come to make me certain
of his treasure and mine,
he will come as relief
of his pain and mine,

he will come, maybe he is coming already:
his whisper.

(Clemente Rebora)

God, my Friend,
this day is yours.
I offer you my acceptance
of whatever you send —
suffering, joy, toil, trouble —
ennobled far beyond my means
because it comes through the greatest gift
you gave me to offer,
Jesus, your Son, our Eucharist.
I pray not to change your mind,
only to understand it,
to yield to it.
But I do ask you to be with me,
especially in....
And I ask your loving watchfulness
for my friend....
Help me find you, through the day,
beneath all your surprising disguises.
Amen.

DAYTIME

Living God,   Presence
I know I overestimate my sins
and thus exaggerate my own importance.
I ask your help to be humble,
not only to admit my faults
but to accept forgiveness.

Abba, let me let you be God.   Grace

Creator God,   Psalm
the sound of your name echoes in all you made.
The gurgling of infants says your name: "I am."
Sighing trees, summer lightning, snow: "I am."
I look to the stars you flamed and set in space,
flickering like fireflies, the burnished moon: "I am."

67

Ah, what are we that you spare a thought for us,
these afterthoughts you seem to dote upon so much?
You summoned scullery folk to be your peers,
made us your regents over this Grand Carouse,
fashioned us to outlast the moon and stars.
How could so wise a God settle for such as we?
Our task is to be grateful, not to understand.
Help us to echo, too, your name: "I am."

(Psalm 8)

Hymn

Love bade me welcome; yet my soul drew back
    Guilty of dust and sin.
But quick-ey'd Love, observing me grow slack
    From my first entrance in,
Drew nearer to me, sweetly questioning
    If I lack'd anything.

"A guest," I answer'd, "worthy to be here";
Love said, "You shall be he."
    "I, the unkind, ungrateful? Ah, my dear,
    I cannot look on Thee."
Love took my hand, and smiling did reply,
    "Who made the eyes but I?"

"Truth, Lord; but I have marr'd them; let my shame
Go where it doth deserve."
"And know you not," says Love, "who bore the blame?"
    "My dear, then I will serve."
"You must sit down," says Love, "and taste My meat."
So I did sit and eat.

(George Herbert)

Reading

I have of late — but wherefore I know not — lost all my mirth,
forgone all custom of exercises; and indeed, it goes so heavily
with my disposition that this goodly frame, the earth, seems
to me a sterile promontory; this most excellent canopy, the
air, look you, this brave o'erhanging firmament, this majes-
tical roof fretted with golden fire — why, it appeareth no
other thing to me than a foul and pestilent congregation of
vapors. What a piece of work is a man! how noble in reason!
how infinite in faculties! in form and moving how express

and admirable! in action how like an angel! in apprehension how like a god! the beauty of the world, the paragon of animals! And yet to me what is this quintessence of dust?

(William Shakespeare)

I thank Christ Jesus our Lord, who is my strength, who judged me worthy of this work, even though I once spoke evil of him and did evil and was evil. But God was merciful to me — because I didn't understand and didn't know what I was doing. And the graciousness of the Lord filled me with the trust and love which comes to us from union with Christ. Here is a saying on which you can ground your very life: Christ Jesus came to cry amnesty to sinners! Who is greater proof of that than I? I was the very worst of sinners! And if God showed mercy to me, I think it was to prove how inexhaustible his patience is. As an example to all of you who must trust him in order to find inexhaustible life.

(1 Timothy 1:12-17)

God, my Friend,
let not the humbug and hypocrisy,
the blabber and blather and baloney all around me
blind and deafen me
to the great shining purpose
underneath it all.
Amen.

Living God,
it is so good —
in fact, essential for my soul —
to close my doors, my ears, my mind,
to anyone or anything
but you.

Abba, it may be a sad song, but make me sing.

Psalm | By the rivers of Babylon we sat us down and wept,
surrendering our harps to the hands of weeping willows.
They plucked the strings and whispered, "Sing! Sing
of the yesteryears when you were young!"
How can I sing of the days when I was whole?
How can I sing in this unfocused wilderness?
How can I sing when the well of my heart is cracked
and barren of pity, even for myself?
Lord, I will take the harp of my soul into my hands.
I will turn suffering to music, and I will sing!

(Psalm 137)

Hymn | I am! Yet what I am who cares, or knows?
My friends forsake me like a memory lost.
I am the self-consumer of my woes,
They rise and vanish in oblivious host,
Like shades in love and death's oblivion lost;
And yet I am, and live with shadows tost.

Into the nothingness of scorn and noise,
Into the living sea of waking dreams,
Where there is neither sense of life nor joys,
But the vast shipwreck of my life's esteems;
And e'en the dearest — that I loved the best —
Are strange — nay, rather stranger than the rest.

I long for scenes where man has never trod,
A place where woman never smiled or wept;
There to abide with my Creator, God,
And sleep as I in childhood sweetly slept:
Untroubling and untroubled where I lie —
The grass below — above the vaulted sky.

(John Clare)

Closing | Holy Friend,
for the next few hours
I entrust the tiller
to your knowing hands.
Amen.

Day Twelve

Presence

Living God,
by now I'm perplexedly aware
of your penchant for paradox,
and one of your more puzzling is that
you want me both docile and decisive.
I'd like some help with that.

Grace

Abba, show me your will, and I'll take it from there.

Psalm

O Lord, my God, you live in a tent made of light.
The clouds are your chariots, borne on wings of wind.
You wrapped the earth in a blue mantle of seas,
holding the waters in check or sending them leaping!
Your life cascades into valleys, gurgles in streams,
siren-songs the animals to slake their thirst,
soaking fields, becoming bread and wine.
Dutifully, the moon arises and the sun retires;
the animals rise and claim their food from you.
At dawn, they slouch toward sleep, and we arise
to claim our living wage from your loving hand.
Should you eclipse your face, where shall we turn?
If you but breathe, fresh life begins in us.
But God, I am not mist or grist or beast.
You cursed-gifted me with a mind to find your will.
I would be dutiful — if you'd but show the way.

(Psalm 104)

Hymn

Ah, my dear angry Lord,
Since thou dost love, yet strike;
Cast down, yet help afford;
Sure I will do the like.

I will complain, yet praise;
I will bewail, approve;
And all my sour-sweet days
I will lament, and love.

(George Herbert)

Offering

God, my friend,
this day is yours.
I offer you my acceptance
of whatever you send —
suffering, joy, toil, trouble —
ennobled far beyond my means
because it comes through the greatest gift
you gave me to offer,
Jesus, your Son, our Eucharist.
I pray not to change your mind,
only to understand it,
to yield to it.
But I do ask you to be with me,
especially in....
And I ask your loving watchfulness
for my friend....
Help me find you, through the day,
beneath all your surprising disguises.
Amen.

DAYTIME

Presence

Living God,
if I am to live as Jesus did, that means
not merely healing the needy but
putting up with pigheaded vested interests,
shamelessly shaming hypocrites,
going on alone, deserted by friends.
If you have that confidence in me,
you'd best give me more confidence in myself.

Abba, give me the courage to make a difference.

He was not what any one of us could have expected:
less than ordinary, nothing stately or attractive,
a man of sorrows, with pain dogging his heels,
the kind of chap you look upon and wince.
People spurned him and wished he'd go away.
Yet the burden of blame he bore was, rightly, ours.
All the while, we sneered, "It serves him right!"
when it was our sins that opened up his wounds,
our sins that flayed the hide from his bones.
Through his punishment we came to peace with God;
as they tore his flesh, our wounds began to heal.
We had strayed like goats, and he became our scapegoat,
mute, like a lamb prodded to the slaughterhouse,
empty-eyed, like a sheep, stupid in the shearer's grip.
He took it all, and he never mumbled a word.

(Isaiah 53:3-7)

I hereby swear that to uphold your house
I would lay my bones in quick destroying lime
Or turn my flesh to timber for all time;
Cut down my womanhood; lop off the boughs
Of that perpetual ecstasy that grows
From the heart's core; condemn it as a crime
If it be broader than a beam, or climb
Above the stature that your roof allows.

I am not the hearthstone nor the cornerstone
Within this noble fabric you have builded;
Not by my beauty was its cornice gilded;
Not on my courage were its arches thrown:
My lord, adjudge my strength, and set me where
I bear a little more than I can bear.

(Elinor Wylie)

Here is how fiat "thy will be done" transforms suffering. To die to self and what self wants is the essence of suffering. If I want x and I get y instead, I suffer, both because I do not get x, which I want, and also because I get y, which I do not want. But if I want only God's will, I do not suffer, because I always get God's will. We suffer to the extent that we are out of line with reality, ultimate reality, God's will. Thus, paradoxically, the essence of suffering (death to self-will) can become its opposite (perfect joy) when it is undertaken freely for love of God. God not only compensates us for suffering, he turns suffering itself into perfect joy if only we obey his first and greatest commandment wholeheartedly, if we only love and will and worship him alone and above all.

(Peter Kreeft)

Scripture | Then Jesus went with them to a grove called Gethsemane, and he said to them, "Stay here awhile. I'm going over there to pray." And he took Peter, James, and John aside a bit, and a terrible sadness suffused his face. "The sorrow in my soul is overwhelming me. Stay here and keep awake with me."

And he went still further off alone and fell to the ground and prayed. "My Father," he moaned. "Please, if it is possible, take this cup of anguish away. But...not what I want. What you want."

After a while, he arose and trudged back to the three. They were asleep. He shook Peter. "You three," he said. "Couldn't you three watch with me even an hour? Stay awake. Pray you won't be put to the test. Yes, I know. The spirit is willing. The flesh is weak."

He went back a second time and fell to his knees: "Father! If this — if this cup of anguish can't be put away unless I drink it, then — as you will."

He came back again and found them sleeping, for their eyes had grown too heavy.

He stumbled back and prayed yet a third time, with the same words, and awhile later he came back again and found them still asleep. "Well, sleep on," he said. "Take your rest. For now is the hour for the Son of Man to be betrayed."

(Matthew 26:36-45)

God, my Friend,
who could count the number of times
I've said the Our Father,
how many times I've so incautiously said,
"Thy will be done"?
Help me say it now and mean it:
not my will, thy will be done.
Amen.

Living God,
you have accepted me —
for reasons only you can understand.
I would be grateful for the humility
to love myself as you love me.

Abba, keep me honest with myself.

Be quick to listen, slow to speak, even-tempered. Hotheaded-
ness never served the cause of God. Test every choice by the
norm the Lord has given: "By their fruits you will know
them."

   Does the choice lead to freedom or chains? You must not
listen to the Word and deceive yourselves, twisting terms,
jimmying loopholes, swindling God. To listen and not obey
is to see your face flat-on in a mirror, then walk away and
forget. But those who stare straight at the taxing truth and
make truth a habit — not just in mind or mouth but in hands
— will finally know what happiness truly means.

   You cannot be honestly religious and deceive yourself.
Genuine religion in the eyes of God is this: do not be seduced
by the World's distorting mirrors; break the mirrors so that
you can truly see.

(James 1:19-27)

True words are not beautiful;
Beautiful words are not true.
A good man does not argue;
He who argues is not a good man.
A wise man has no extensive knowledge;

75

He who has extensive knowledge is not a wise man.
The sage does not accumulate for himself.
The more he uses for others, the more he has for himself.
The more he gives to others,
    the more he possesses of his own.
The Way of Heaven is to benefit others
    and not to injure.
The Way of Heaven is to act but not to compete.

(Lao-tzu)

Closing | Holy Friend,
if the Chinese sage is correct,
and confusion is a sure sign of wisdom,
there is a better than even chance
I might be wise.
Thank you.
Amen.

Day Thirteen

Living God,
you've given me one more chance again.
Help me pick up the puzzling pieces
and try to create a day
worthy of us both.

Presence

Abba, calm all my unfounded qualms.

Grace

Whoever dwells in the shelter of the Most High God
need have no fear of snares or terrors in the night,
of the slings and arrows of outrageous folk or fortune,
of plagues that stalk the dark or howl at noon.
They can scourge your flesh but never touch your soul,
mock your faith but not besmirch your name.
Though a thousand fall, left and right, you will endure
with soul unsullied and your name secure in your hands.
"I stand with all who persevere with me.
I champion not the brave but the unbowed.
I cheer the hearts of cowards who stand firm.
I will use such souls to show how I can save."

(Psalm 91)

Psalm

Consider when thou art moved to be wroth,
He who was God and of all men the best,
Seeing Himself scorned and scourged both,
And as a thief between two thieves threst,
With all rebuke and shame; yet from His breast
Came never sign of wrath or of disdain,
But patiently endured all the pain.

Hymn

Think on the very lamentable pain,
Think on the piteous cross of woeful Christ,
Think on His blood beat out at every vein,
Think on His precious heart carved in twain;
Think how for thy redemption all was wrought,
Let Him not lose what He so dear hath bought.
(Pico della Mirandola, Tr. Thomas More)

Offering

God, my Friend,
this day is yours.
I offer you my acceptance
of whatever you send —
suffering, joy, toil, trouble —
ennobled far beyond my means
because it comes through the greatest gift
you gave me to offer,
Jesus, your Son, our Eucharist.
I pray not to change your mind,
only to understand it,
to yield to it.
But I do ask you to be with me,
especially in....
And I ask your loving watchfulness
for my friend....
Help me find you, through the day
beneath all your surprising disguises.
Amen.

DAYTIME

Presence

Living God,
it seems fulfillment
is always somewhere in the future,
a sense of accomplishment that will come...some day.
Well, if it's all right with you,
I'd like to be content with today.

Grace

Abba, crack open all that's locked in me.

Psalm

Lord, you see to the roots of my blood and bones.
You eavesdrop on every thought and dream I have.

If I stand or sit or lay me down, you are there.
If I burrow into the darkest dark, you are there.
If I fly to the gates of dawn, you're there before,
behind, within, beyond, above, below.
At times, I resent your callousness to privacy,
and yet…and yet without you I am alone.
I thank you for the wonder of myself.
Examine me and know my inmost heart,
and when I meet you there, I will break out,
out of this labyrinth into forever.

(Psalm 139)

In heaven   **Hymn**
Some little blades of grass
Stood before God.
"What did you do?"
Then all save one of the little blades
Began eagerly to relate
The merits of their lives.
This one stayed a small way behind,
Ashamed.
Presently, God said,
"And what did you do?"
The little blade answered, "Oh, my Lord,
Memory is bitter to me,
For, if I did good deeds,
I know not of them."
Then God, in all his splendor,
Arose from his throne.
"Oh, best little blade of grass!" he said.

(Stephen Crane)

Be content that you are not yet a saint, even though you   **Reading**
realize that the only thing worth living for is sanctity. Then
you will be satisfied to let God lead you to sanctity by paths
that you cannot understand. You will travel in darkness in
which you will no longer be concerned with yourself and no
longer compare yourself with others. Those who have gone
by that way have finally found out that sanctity is in everything and that God is all around them. Having given up all
desire to compete with others they suddenly wake up and

find that the joy of God is everywhere, and they are able to exult in the virtues and goodness of others more than they ever could have done in their own.

(Thomas Merton)

Scripture	Good times and bad times, I've seen them all, and I'm here. I've learned to manage on whatever God gives me. I know how to get along when I'm poor; I know how to get along when I have more than enough. In my initiation, I got down to the bedrock truth, so I'm ready for anything, anywhere, full belly or empty, poverty or plenty. There is nothing — nothing whatever — I can't endure, as long as I'm not alone, as long as I feel the presence of the One who gives me strength.

(Philippians 4:11-14)

Closing	God, my Friend, if you could only convince me to let go of the search for certitudes, I'd be fine. Amen.

EVENING

Presence	Living God, in the world outside this silent space, everything rages, roars, clamors for attention. At last, here in this silence, convince me to prefer peace.
Grace	Abba, just keep me hangin' on!
Psalm	The rivers rage, O Lord, and my boat is small. Rebellion thunders round my thin-shelled soul, and cataracts of noise crack in the darksome night. I fear that my skiff will founder in waves like cliffs. God, blow on my flicker of faith and make it burn.

Make me cling not to what I fear but to what I know:
that my God is from forever to forever firm,
an unshakable bulwark against the battering seas,
a beacon to cleave impenetrable storms,
the harbor to which you faithfully lead me home.

(Psalm 93)

My soul, there is a country   **Hymn**
   Far beyond the stars,
Where stands a winged sentry
   All skilful in the wars:
There, above noise and danger
   Sweet Peace sits crowned with smiles,
And One born in a manger
   Commands the beauteous files.
He is thy gracious friend
   And — O my soul, awake! —
Did in pure love descend
   To die here for thy sake.
If thou canst get but thither,
   There grows the flower of Peace,
The Rose that cannot wither,
   Thy fortress, and thy ease.
Leave then thy foolish ranges
   For none can thee secure,
But one who never changes,
   Thy God, thy life, thy cure.

(Henry Vaughan)

Holy Friend,   **Closing**
I just blew out my breath,
all the in-charge-ness that
I've carried around all day.
Whew!
Over to you!
And out.
Amen.

Day Fourteen

Presence | Living God,
all round me voices bellow,
"Nothing succeeds like the appearance of success."
Help me to cling to substance over surface,
honesty over acceptance,
truth over trivial froth.
Oh, I need help, all right.

Grace | Abba, ransom me. I can't do it alone.

Psalm | Why should I fear when misfortune dogs my heels?
Some hope to ransom their lives with their wealth,
but only a fool could say, "I redeem myself!"
And who would cancel the debt? Only himself.
Some will take money in exchange for their souls.
But who could ever collect them? Only Death.
Fools die, on the whole, as often as the wise,
and their heirs gobble the only value they had.
"This above all: to thine own self be true!"
has a spurious ring of wisdom to it, at first,
but an awesome echo of loneliness in the end.
True-to-oneself is a trivial kind of truth.
No, I trust no one as disposable as my self.
No matter what the price, I trust in God:
My Rock. My assurance. My Redeemer.

(Psalm 49)

Hymn | O, how much more doth beauty beauteous seem
By that sweet ornament which truth doth give!
The rose looks fair, but fairer we it deem

82

For that sweet odour which doth in it live.
The canker-blooms have full as deep a dye
As the perfumed tincture of the roses,
Hang on such thorns, and play as wantonly
When summer's breath their masked buds discloses:
But for their virtue only is their show,
They live unwoo'd and unrespected fade;
Die to themselves. Sweet roses do not so;
Of their sweet deaths are sweetest odours made.
   And so of you, beauteous and lovely youth,
   When that shall evade, my verse distills your truth.
(William Shakespeare)

Offering

God, my Friend,
this day is yours.
I offer you my acceptance
of whatever you send —
suffering, joy, toil, trouble —
ennobled far beyond my means
because it comes through the greatest gift
you gave me to offer,
Jesus, your Son, our Eucharist.
I pray not to change your mind,
only to understand it,
to yield to it.
But I do ask you to be with me,
especially in....
And I ask your loving watchfulness
for my friend....
Help me find you, through the day,
beneath all your surprising disguises.
Amen.

DAYTIME

Presence

Living God,
I balk at the word *saint*.
Yet Paul says the title is our birthright in Christ.
Is it possible that Paul was more freed
and wiser
than I?

83

Grace | Abba, assure me. My self-assurance is shaky.

Psalm | Charmed by their beauty, fools take things for gods,
so enraptured by the art, they ignore the Artisan.
If creation crackles with power, what is its Source?
If only the Author knows how the story will end,
and none of us knows even what the next chapter brings,
then whose hand unrolls the scrolls of our lives?

But small blame to those who revel in God's creation
with children's hearts, heedless of their Creator,
victims of appearances, seeing so much to enjoy.
Far greater chance for them than for the self-assured
that one day God will open the eyes of their eyes
and reveal himself, blazing beneath the surfaces
of everything we see and touch and feel and love.

(Wisdom 13:3-9)

Hymn | God moves in a mysterious way,
    His wonders to perform;
He plants his footsteps in the sea,
    And rides upon the storm.

Ye fearful saints fresh courage take;
The clouds ye so much dread
Are big with mercy, and shall break
In blessings on your head.

Judge not the Lord by feeble sense,
    But trust him for his grace;
Behind a frowning providence,
    He hides a smiling face.

His purposes will ripen fast,
    Unfolding ev'ry hour;
The bud may have a bitter taste,
    But sweet will be the flow'r.

Blind unbelief is sure to err,
  And scan his work in vain;
God is his own interpreter,
  And he will make it plain.

(William Cowper)

Reading

We may observe that the teaching of our Lord himself, in which there is no imperfection, is not given us in that cut-and-dried, fool-proof, systematic fashion we might have expected or desired. He wrote no book. We have only reported sayings, most of them uttered in answer to questions, shaped in some degree by their context. And when we have collected them all we cannot reduce them to a system. He preaches but He does not lecture. He uses paradox, proverb, exaggeration, parable, irony even (I mean no irreverence) the "wisecrack." He utters maxims which, like popular proverbs, if rigorously taken, may seem to contradict one another. His teaching therefore cannot be grasped by the intellect alone, cannot be "got up" as if it were a "subject." If we try to do that with it, we shall find Him the most elusive of teachers. He hardly ever gave a straight answer to a straight question. He will not be, in the way we want, "pinned down." The attempt is (again, I mean no irreverence) like trying to bottle a sunbeam.

(C.S. Lewis)

Scripture

The disciples went up to Jesus and said, "Why do you talk all the time in parables? Can't you speak plain?" And Jesus smiled. "The mysteries are revealed to the open heart, not to the open mind. An obtuse mind is better than an obtuse heart. Those who are humble enough to accept the gift of the Kingdom will have kingdoms and kingdoms more. Those who are too arrogant to accept any gift, will be impoverished down to their own self-importance."

(Matthew 13:10-13)

Closing | God, my Friend,
I've been too busy and too self-important
to revel in anything innocent recently.
I'm sure there's something out there
waiting to deliver me joy.
Help me not to be too grown-up
to enjoy it.
Amen.

EVENING

Presence | Living God,
my body seems so palpable and permanent,
and my soul — my self — so elusive and well...
frankly...unmarketable.
Oh, undeceive me on that one!
Don't let me sell my soul
like some ratty old antique
I'm too busy to appraise.

Grace | Abba, tell me I'm worth picking up and starting over.

Psalm | God, I often stumble into envying the smug,
the sleek and sly, the arrogantly disdainful,
their skins too thick to suffer grief or doubt,
their hearts as sensitive to pain as arrowheads.
They wear their hubris like a chain of gold
and swathe themselves in icy callousness.
People admire their toughness and their drive,
their swagger, their cool and cocky contempt for you.
Am I fool to cling to my integrity?
Is it for nothing that I go on trusting you,
when you seem, at least, to betray me every hour?

But the bitter blindness melted like a dream at dawn,
and I saw the emptiness within their armor,
the soulless shells shambling in the dark.
Within my indocile body and my unruly mind,
you dwell at my inmost center like a flame,
a compass drawn home through darkness into light.

(Psalm 73)

Thou art indeed just, Lord, if I contend
With thee; but, sir, so what I plead is just.
Why do sinners' ways prosper? and why must
Disappointment all I endeavour end?
   Wert thou my enemy, O thou my friend,
How wouldst thou worse, I wonder, than thou dost
Defeat, thwart me? Oh, the sots and thralls of lust
Do in spare hours more thrive than I that spend,
Sir, life upon thy cause. See, banks and brakes
Now, leaved how thick! Laced they are again
With fretly chervil, look, and fresh wind shakes
Them; birds build — but not I build; no, but strain,
Time's eunuch, and not breed one work that wakes.
Mine, O thou lord of life, send my roots rain.
                              (Gerard Manley Hopkins)

Holy Friend,
now that I've gotten that out of my system —
and I'm grateful that you listened —
let me leave the perks of the prominent behind
and be content with who I am,
what I've done,
and you.
Amen.

Day Fifteen

Presence

Living God,
grant me the serenity to accept
the things that can't be changed,
the courage to change what can be changed,
and the wisdom to know the difference.

Grace

Abba, help me face all the little deaths, unafraid.

Psalm

Coward that I was, I held my tongue
and called it shyness, reticence, reserve —
even in the face of arrant wickedness.
But some spark of honor smoldered in my heart,
and the words blundered out: "My life is too short
to cower in servile silence like a cur!
To walk transparent and dismissable as air!"
God, you have given me a pinch or two of life.
Then let me use it as you would have me do.
Breathe your fiery Spirit into me.
Take me in hand and point me on the way.
Make me not an aimless wanderer but a pilgrim!
My purpose is not merely to survive but live!

(Psalm 39)

Hymn

Do not go gentle into that good night,
Old age should burn and rave at close of day;
Rage, rage against the dying of the light.

88

Though wise men at their end know dark is right,
Because their words had forked no lightning they
Do not go gentle into that good night....

Wild men who caught and sang the sun in flight,
And learn, too late, then, grieved it on its way,
Do not go gentle into that good night.

Grave men, near death, who see with blinding sight
Blind eyes could blaze like meteors and be gay,
Rage, rage against the dying of the light.

And you, my father, there on the sad height,
Curse, bless, me now with your fierce tears, I pray.
Do not go gentle into that good night.
Rage, rage against the dying of the light.

(Dylan Thomas)

Offering

God, my Friend,
this day is yours.
I offer you my acceptance
of whatever you send —
suffering, joy, toil, trouble —
ennobled far beyond my means
because it comes through the greatest gift
you gave me to offer,
Jesus, your Son, our Eucharist.
I pray not to change your mind,
only to understand it,
to yield to it.
But I do ask you to be with me,
especially in....
And I ask your loving watchfulness
for my friend....
Help me find you, through the day,
beneath all your surprising disguises.
Amen.

Presence	Living God, I'm sick of being measured. "My, my, we're doing better today!" Can't we all just leave yesterday behind and get on with it?
Grace	Abba, let me not be too proud to share my pain or too humble to share others'.
Psalm	My flesh rebels; my guts are feverish with fear, numbed and crushed. Sometimes I moan aloud. The others seldom notice, but, my Lord, my sighing is no secret hid from you. My friends come by, revulsion in their smiles. Even the dearest keep a distance in their eyes. Ones I thought my friends seem to have moved away. Father, forgive them their helplessness to know. When they have gone, and you and I are left alone, keep whispering to me over and over, "Courage, friend! This puzzling pain can stir their hearts to care and turn to me. Helpless or not, they are there." <div align="right">(Psalm 38)</div>
Hymn	When we our betters see bearing our woes, We scarcely think our miseries our foes. Who alone suffers, suffers most i' the mind, Leaving free things and happy shows behind; But when the mind much sufferance doth o'erskip When grief hath mates, and bearing fellowship, How light and portable my pain seems now, When that which makes me bend makes the King bow, He childed as I fathered! <div align="right">(William Shakespeare)</div>
Reading	In the first legend of the Grail, it is said that the Grail (the miraculous vessel that satisfies all hunger by virtue of the consecrated Host) belongs to the first comer who asks the guardian of the vessel, a king three-quarters paralyzed by the most painful wound, "What are you going through?"

The love of our neighbor in all its fullness simply means being able to say to him: "What are you going through?" It is a recognition that the sufferer exists, not only as a unit in a collection, or a specimen from the social category labeled "unfortunate," but as a man, exactly like us, who was one day stamped with a special mark by affliction. For this reason it is enough, but it is indispensable, to know how to look at him in a certain way. The soul empties itself of all its own contents in order to receive into itself the being it is looking at, just as he is, in all his truth.

(Simone Weil)

| | Scripture |

If someone you know misbehaves and you are kind enough to try to set him or her right, be sure to do it in the spirit of gentleness — for you yourself will sometimes misbehave. To fulfill the law of Christ, we must share one another's burdens. Oddly enough, it is people who fancy themselves important who are really not. Before you judge others' conduct, judge your own. If you have done something good, be rightly proud of it — all by itself — not because it is better than what your neighbor has done. We are glad of help, but in the end we each carry our own.

(Galatians 6:1-5)

Closing

God, my Friend,
as I hope for compassion,
give me the graciousness
to get inside the skins of others
and walk around in them awhile.
Amen.

EVENING

Presence

Living God,
others have passed judgment on my day,
most of them far in excess of the cause,
whether to praise or blame.
I'd appreciate perspective
to see today as a whole.

Abba, give me peace for now, challenges tomorrow.

Grace

Psalm	As the doe roams in search of crystal streams,
	so my soul roves in quest of you, my God,
	not utterly without hope, not utterly without doubt.
	Where can I turn, then, and know I will see your face?
	The cynics round me snicker, "Credulous fool!
	You pay for your luck with your licks,
	and that's all there's to it."
	I block my ears, but my soul still listens.
	Why am I so heartsore, if I truly trust in you?
	I do. But put spine into my fragile, faltering faith.
	Blow on the graying embers of my hope.
	Weed the doubt and fear from my brambled brain.
	Then I will set out on my quest for you again,
	and the journey itself will be my prayer, my God.

(Psalm 42)

Hymn	Oh! Mary, Oh! Marthy, go tell my disciples,
	Gwine-a meet Him in Gallalee,
	Gwine-a meet Him in Gallalee.
	Yes, bless de Lawd, meet Him in Gallalee.
	Gwine-a meet Him in Gallalee.
	Oh! yondah come duh charet,
	Duh hosses dressed in white,
	Duh fo' wheels a runnin' by duh grace ob God,
	An' duh hin' wheels a runnin' by love;
	An' duh hin' wheels a runnin' by love.
	Oh! yondah come Brudder Peter,
	An' how do you know it's him?
	Wid a crown upon his fo'head
	An' de keys of Bethlyham,
	An' de keys of Bethlyham.
	Yes, bless de Lawd, keys of Bethlyham;
	An' de keys of Bethlyham.

Oh! yondah come Sista Mary,
An' how do you know it's huhr?
A shoutin' Hallelujah
An' praises to duh Lamb,
An' praises to duh Lamb.
Yes, bless de Lawd, praises to duh Lamb;
An' praises to duh Lamb.

(an unknown black poet)

Holy Friend,   **Closing**
I offer what I've done today,
the minor mistakes and minor joys.
All in all, I'm satisfied.
And I pray that you are, too.
Amen.

Day Sixteen

Presence
Living God,
refine my vision today.
Let me focus the faces I pass every day
and never see.
Make me aware of the crevices of my room,
the "specially chosen junk"
and what once made it all precious,
the good times.

Grace
Abba, shock me with all I fail to see.

Psalm
Anyone with a voice to sing, shout for joy!
Wipe off your solemn faces and grab a harp!
Stop squinting at all your troubles and look around!
We live on a turquoise jewel in a sea of stars,
amid the heavenly carouse the Lord has made.
The ocean harrumphs on the shore, the wind keens
through the trees, streams chuckle, geysers hoot,
and valleys reverberate it back again
in a great, wild, symphonic hymn of praise!

How can you squat there grimly awaiting doom
when this circus of sound is soaring all about you?
How can you cocoon yourself in your woeful shell
when the whole rest of creation reels in a dance?
How can you pick over your woes like a miser with coins
when the Lord of the Dance has made you only to live?
(Psalm 33)

What is this life, if, full of care,
We have no time to stand and stare.

No time to stand beneath the boughs
And stare as long as sheep or cows.

No time to see, in broad daylight,
Streams full of stars, like skies at night.

No time to turn at Beauty's glance,
And watch her feet, how they can dance.

No time to wait till her mouth can
Enrich that smile her eyes began.

A poor life this if, full of care,
We have no time to stand and stare.

(William Henry Davies)

God, my Friend,
this day is yours.
I offer you my acceptance
of whatever you send —
suffering, joy, toil, trouble —
ennobled far beyond my means
because it comes through the greatest gift
you gave me to offer,
Jesus, your Son, our Eucharist.
I pray not to change your mind,
only to understand it,
to yield to it.
But I do ask you to be with me,
especially in....
And I ask your loving watchfulness
for my friend....
Help me find you, through the day,
beneath all your surprising disguises.
Amen.

DAYTIME

Presence | Living God,
remind me of Annie Sullivan,
drawing signs
in Helen Keller's resentful, uncomprehending hands.
As you did with me.
As now you send me to do.

Grace | Abba, make me heal myself by healing others.

Psalm | Mischievous God, you duped, deceived, seduced me!
In giving me freedom, you allowed me to act the fool.
Made in your image, I assumed I was made your peer.
But you are stronger, and inescapable,
  and you finally brought me to my knees,
the only place to see who I really am:
your servant, healer, sent to set them free.

But there you duped, deceived, seduced me again!
As I did, they think that they are already free!
Free to do whatever, whenever, they choose.
"We can do quite well without your God," they sneer.
"You're young only once, so grab all the gusto you can!
Spoilsport puritans! Times have changed. Get lost!"

Lord, being a prophet is not a job I'd have chosen.
I deafen myself to your call, but it does no good!
Surely there are others more glib and charming than I,
more patient, unflappable, Teflon-skinned.
Why not consider offering this challenge to them?
But always the same reply: "No. I want you."

(Jeremiah 20:7-13)

Hymn | Oh, Jesus walked this lonesome valley.
He had to walk it for his-sef.
'Cause nobody else
Can walk it for you.
You have to walk it
By yo'self.

When you face that Judgmunt mawnin',
You got to face it by yo'sef;
'Cause nobody else
Can face it faw you.
You got to face it
By yo'self.

When my dear Lawd was hangin' bleedin',
He had to hang tha by His-sef;
'Cause nobody else
Could hang tha faw Him.
He had to hang tha
By His'sef.

You got to live a life of service,
You got to live it by yo'sef;
'Cause nobody heah
To live it faw you.
You got to live it
By yo'sef.

(an unknown black poet)

Reading

If we lived in a State where virtue was profitable, common sense would make us good, and greed would make us saintly. And we'd live like animals or angels in the happy land that *needs* no heroes. But since in fact we see that avarice, anger, envy, pride, sloth, lust and stupidity commonly profit far beyond humility, chastity, fortitude, justice and thought, and have to choose, to be human at all...why then perhaps we *must* stand fast a little — even at the risk of being heroes.
(Robert Bolt)

Scripture

When Simon saw the boats so awash with fish they were about to founder, he fell to his knees before Jesus. "Lord!" he stammered. "You'd best leave me. I am a sinful man." For he and his mates and his partners, James and John, were numbstruck at the catch they'd made.

But Jesus smiled at Simon. "No, no! Don't be afraid. From now on, it's souls I'll send you out to catch!" Then, beaching their boats...they set out on the road with him.
(Luke 5:8-11)

Closing | God, my Friend,
in the past, just as Simon,
I never saw myself as anyone special.
I was netted in my own problems,
my shortcomings, my sins.
Now I get unnerving hints
you want me to use those nets
for something else.
Amen.

EVENING

Presence | Living God,
perhaps...no, of course you do know
that in drag races they strip the cars
to the absolute essentials and no more
so the cars can get where they're going faster.
...I wish now I hadn't reminded you of that.

Grace | Abba, make me want more than I want to want.

Psalm | To the end of my days, let my life give praise to God!
He has freed me from my fears! Healed my helplessness!
Taste and see how sweet is his graciousness.
If you want to know fulfillment, forget yourself,
and come out on the road to find the Prince of Peace.
Leave all your excess baggage by the side of the road:
malice, bruisable feelings, envy, grudges,
and there, at the top of the pile, leave fear.
Oh, there are hardships aplenty on the path ahead,
but wherever we encounter heartbreak, we encounter God.
And no one can capture our souls along the way,
for the Prince already gave himself in ransom,
and with free hearts we have nothing left to pay.

(Psalm 34)

I heard the sound of the Gospel train,
Don't you want to get on? Yes, that's my aim.
I'll stand at the station an' patiently wait
For the train that's comin', an' she's never late.
You must have your ticket stamped bright an' clear,
Train is comin', she's drawin' near.

It keeps me always in a move an' strain,
Tryin' to be ready for the Gospel train.
Ever now an' then, either day or night,
I examine my ticket to see if I'm right.
If the Son grant my ticket the Holy Ghost sign,
Then there is no way to be left behind.

There's a great deal of talk 'bout the Judgment Day,
You have no time for to trifle away.
I'll tell you one thing certain an' sho',
Judgment Day's comin' when you don't know.
I hope to be ready when I'm called to go,
If anything's lackin', Lawd, let me know.

                              (an unknown black poet)

Holy Friend,   **Closing**
I hope to be ready when I'm called to go,
If anything's lackin', Lawd,
let me know.
Amen.

Day Seventeen

Presence | Living God,
you are everywhere,
but I'm here-and-now;
your knowing is all-encompassing,
but mine is step by step.
Have I warned you
what you're dealing with?

Grace | Abba, I'm not ready at all, Coach. But send me in!

Psalm | The vault of heaven sings with the glory of God!
One day chatters the age-old news to the next,
and tonight passes the word on to tomorrow.
No noise, mind you; no word you or I could hear,
deafened as we are to the sounds of silence.
And yet their message echoes in the depths of the sea,
rolls through the valleys and up the mountainsides:
"God in heaven has pitched a tent for the sun!
He strides from the pavilion like a bridegroom
    seeking his love,
Like a sprinter, shivering in readiness
    to begin his race.
God's Son is a healer! Let all the earth sing praise!"

(Psalm 19)

Hymn | As I in hoary winter's night
    stood shivering in the snow,
Surprised I was with sudden heat
    which made my heart to glow;
And lifting up a fearful eye

100

to view what fire was near,
A pretty Babe all burning bright
   did in the air appear;
Who, scorched with excessive heat,
   such floods of tears did shed,
As though his floods should quench his flames
   which with his tears were fed.
"Alas!" quoth he, "but newly born
   in fiery heats I fry,
Yet none approach to warm their hearts
   or feel my fire but I.
My faultless breast the furnace is;
   the fuel, wounding thorns;
Love is the fire, and sighs the smoke,
   the ashes shame and scorns;
The fuel justice layeth on,
   and mercy blows the coals;
The metal in this furnace wrought
   are men's defiled souls:
For which, as now on fire
   I am to work them to their good,
So will I melt into a bath
   to wash them in my blood."
With this he vanished out of sight
   and swiftly shrunk away,
And straight I called unto mind
   that it was Christmas day.

                                           (Robert Southwell)

Offering

God, my Friend,
this day is yours.
I offer you my acceptance
of whatever you send —
suffering, joy, toil, trouble —
ennobled far beyond my means
because it comes through the greatest gift
you gave me to offer,
Jesus, your Son, our Eucharist.
I pray not to change your mind,
only to understand it,
to yield to it.

But I do ask you to be with me,
especially in....
And I ask your loving watchfulness
for my friend....
Help me find you, through the day,
beneath all your surprising disguises.
Amen.

DAYTIME

Presence

Living God,
for the rest of the day
can we concentrate on "petty"?
Petty complaints, petty jealousies,
petty thieves, petty conceits, petty pet peeves.
Let's roll them up in a big ball
and toss them.

Grace

Abba, let my life be one worth dying for.

Psalm

The upright, though they die too soon, find rest.
Length of life is not a badge of honor;
worthiness is not bestowed for a sentence served.
Those who lived unsoiled among sinners are saved,
for God loves those whose souls remain their own.
The witchery of petty pleasures distorts the truth,
and the whirlwind of desire bewilders simpletons.
But those who keep their eyes on God alone
have found fulfillment, no matter how brief their stay.
Yet others watch and do not understand
that God is not impressed by length of days,
for time, where God abides, is meaningless,
and what we value most is valueless.
Those who watch and sneer at those who trust
in God are unaware that all the while
God is snickering up his sleeve at them.

(Wisdom 4:7-18)

Hymn

Death, be not proud, though some have called thee
Mighty and dreadful, for thou art not so;
For those whom thou thinkest thou dost overthrow

102

Die not, poor Death; nor yet canst thou kill me.
From rest and sleep, which but thy pictures be,
Much pleasure; then from thee much more must flow;
And soonest our best men with thee do go —
Rest of their bones and souls' delivery.
Thou'rt slave to fate, chance, kings,
    and desperate men,
And dost with poison, war, and sickness dwell;
And poppy or charms can make us sleep as well
And better than thy stroke. Why swell'st thou then?
One short sleep past, we wake eternally,
And Death shall be no more: Death, thou shalt die.

(John Donne)

"The Apology of Socrates"

Reading

But you, too, my judges, ought to be of good hope about death and believe that this is true at least: no evil can befall a good man, alive or dead, nor are the gods indifferent to his affairs. What has happened to me is not by chance, because I'm convinced that to die now and be released from worldly cares is the best thing for me. This is why the sign from the gods did not turn me back. Therefore, I bear no malice whatever against those who brought this on me....But now it is time for us to part — I to die, you to live. Which of us goes to the better fate is known to no one — except God.

(Plato)

We are dead to sin; then how can we be in sin for very long? When we were submerged into the waters of baptism, we were submerged into the death of Christ Jesus. For that instant, we were breathless with Jesus in the tomb, joined within that instant, dead and reborn, as Jesus was to the Father's glory.

Scripture

Becoming one with Jesus in that moment's dying, we become one with Jesus into the forever of living. Our former lives were crucified with him and in him, to set us free! Free of the fear of unforgivable sin! And at death now, there can be no fear.

(Romans 6:3-7)

Closing | God, my Friend,
right now I don't really feel super-alive.
But I have to admit, being with you,
I feel more important, more alive,
than any other time today.
Amen.

EVENING

Presence | Living God,
I'm a bit dithery at the end of the day,
like someone off a ship, rubbery-legged,
still cautious not to be thrown this way and that.
Help me to savor awhile
the peace you made me for.

Grace | Abba, since I can't comprehend, give me the graciousness
to be grateful.

Psalm | Within the belly of the great fish, Jonah prayed:
"From the abyss of my anguish, I cried unto the Lord,
and from far away he heard my voice and answered me.
You cast me into the dark heart of the sea,
where the black waters sucked me down and engulfed me.
And I moaned, 'God has cast me from his sight,
    abandoned me!'
Tangled in seaweed, I careened in dark whirlpools,
choking for air, down to the roots of the mountains,
down into the black cavernous cities of the dead.
But, suddenly, in the suffocating dark,
    I remembered my God.
And my prayer rose through the depths: 'I will praise!
I will take up the burden you give me,
    and that will be my prayer!' "

(Jonah 2:1-9)

We think that Paradise and Calvary,
Christ's cross, and Adam's tree, stood in one place;
Look, Lord, and find both Adams met in me;
As the first Adam's sweat surrounds my face,
May the last Adam's blood my soul embrace.
So, in his purple wrapped receive me, Lord,
By these his thorns give me his other crown;
And as to others' souls I preached thy word,
Be this my text, my sermon to mine own,
Therefore that he may raise the Lord throws down.

(John Donne)

Hymn

Holy Friend,
wrapped in this peace of Christ,
I bid you *adieu, adios, a dio* —
if that's not doubly
redundant.
Amen.

Closing

Day Eighteen

Presence

Living God,
as I've said so often before,
the prophet's mantle doesn't fit my shoulders.
It's really a problem for my spine.
When you come down to it…
Ah, yes. I understand.

Grace

Abba, if you help me forget myself, I can.

Psalm

From nowhere, the voice of God came to me, saying:
"Before I rooted you in your mother's womb, I knew you.
Before you were born, I had consecrated your life.
I commissioned you to be a prophet to all humankind!"
I twisted and stammered,
"G-G-G-G-od! Oh, no! No!
See! I can ha-ha-hardly speak! I'm just a child."
And God answered,
"Hush! Do not say you are a child.
Now rise and go. Bring the news to them.
Uproot your dithering fears and cast them off.
I am with you. What right have you to be shy?"

(Jeremiah 1:4-8)

Hymn

A leaf moved up on me, like a tattered
   old sailor dropped from the long winds
    that bend over the hill,
Grey-cheeked, tobacco-browned,
   vaguely musty of cargoes of acorns
    and spider-silks woven in springtimes long dead.

How it tumbled about in a random way,
  stood on its leg of a broken stem,
Rattled a dry throat and lighted an empty pipe
  from a dying ember!

I would have given it a silver shilling,
  but it had no hands,
I would have dropped it safely
  into a warm cavern of quartz,
  but someone was watching,
I would have put it to my eye and seen God,
  while the slow train was belling
  like the cows coming down the lane —
Except that I am a fool.

                                    (Hugh de Burgh)

Offering

God, my Friend,
this day is yours.
I offer you my acceptance
of whatever you send —
suffering, joy, toil, trouble —
ennobled far beyond my means
because it comes through the greatest gift
you gave me to offer,
Jesus, your Son, our Eucharist.
I pray not to change your mind,
only to understand it,
to yield to it.
But I do ask you to be with me,
especially in....
And I ask your loving watchfulness
for my friend....
Help me find you, through the day,
beneath all your surprising disguises.
Amen.

DAYTIME

Presence

Living God,
in our world now, as you know,
domestic servants aren't highly paid — or regarded.

107

Yet, judging from what Jesus did
at the Last Supper,
with that towel and warm water....
Yes, I thought that's what you meant.

Grace Abba, give me a heart that doesn't count the cost.

Psalm Then the King will say to those on his right:
"Come. You are the ones my Father finds fit,
the ones who did not miss the point of it all.
For I was hungry for forgiveness,
   and you gave me food.
I was parched with the need to be needed,
   and you slaked my thirst.
I was lost and alone in the crowd,
   and you took my hand.
I was naked to my tormentors,
   and you covered my shame.
I was sick with corrosive self-pity,
   and you shook me hard.
I was imprisoned in cynical doubts,
   and you never lost patience.
Come. You are the ones my Father finds fit,
   the ones who did not miss the point of it all."

(Matthew 25:34-40)

Hymn   More servants wait on man
Then he'l take notice of: in ev'ry path
   He treads down that which doth befriend him,
   When sickness makes him pale and wan.
Oh, mighty love! Man is one world, and hath
   Another to attend him.

    Since then, my God, thou hast
So brave a Palace built; O dwell in it,
   That it may dwell with thee at last!
   Till then, afford us so much wit;
That, as the world serves us, we may serve thee,
   And both thy servants be.

(George Herbert)

The nations and the classes and the individuals were always crying out, "Mine, mine," where the Church was instructed to say, "Ours." If this were true, then it would not be a question only of sharing property, as such. It would be a question of sharing everything — even thoughts, feelings, lives. God had told people that they would have to cease to live as individuals. They would have to go into the force of life, like a drop falling into a river. God has said that it was only the men who could give up their jealous selves, their futile individualities of happiness and sorrow, who would die peacefully and enter the ring. He that would save his life was asked to lose it.

(T.H. White)

Reading

Jesus knew that, at that moment, the Father had put everything into his hands. So he got up from table, removed his outer garment, and took a towel, wrapping it around his waist. He poured water into a basin and went round the table, washing his friends' feet and wiping them with the towel.

Peter scowled down at him. "Lord, you're not going to wash my feet, are you?" And Jesus said, "Right now, you can't understand what I'm doing. Later, you will." "No!" Peter snapped. "You will never wash my feet!" And Jesus said, "If I don't, we have nothing in common again, you and I." Peter looked at him, puzzled, sadly, and said, "Then, Lord, wash my feet, my hands; wash everything!"..."Do you understand," Jesus asked them, "what I've just done?" They looked around, stupidly. "If you call me Master and Lord," Jesus said, "and if I've just washed your feet, then there's an example for you. When do you begin to wash one another's feet?"

(John 13:4-15)

Scripture

God, my Friend,
unless I misread John's gospel —
and his was the latest written of the four —
there is no explicit reference
to Jesus celebrating the Eucharist,
only this business with the feet.
Could you help me understand
what they have in common?
Amen.

Closing

EVENING

Presence

Living God,
we've spoken...I've spoken
about this prophet thing before.
It's the end of the day,
and I'm not really into challenge just now.
Oh. I see.

Grace

Abba, if you trust me to do it, that's a guarantee.

Psalm

"You are my chosen, in whom my soul delights.
I have infused you with my spirit
    to bring justice to the world.
You must not shout; walk silent through the streets.
You will not crush the weak or shun the fainthearted.
You will give them courage to establish peace on earth.
I, who stretched out the heavens like a tent
and set the world within it like a spinning sapphire,
who breathed life into every living thing on earth,
have called you forth to serve the cause of right.
You are my covenant with the people,
    the light of the world.
Henceforth, you are anointed
    to open the eyes of the blind,
    to clang open the dungeon bars,
    to lead those in darkness into light.
Don't look around! I mean you!"

(Isaiah 42:1-9)

Hymn

You go, I'll go wid you;
Open yo' mouth, I'll speak for you:
Lord, if I go, tell me what to say.
Day won't believe in me.

Now, Lord, I give myself to Thee,
'Tis all dat I can do.
If thou should draw thyself from me,
Oh, wither shall I flee?

De archangels done droop dere wings,
Went up on Zion's hill to sing;
Climbin' Jacob's ladder high,
Gwine reach heab'n by an' by.

(an unknown black poet)

Holy Friend,
you are tireless.
But would you ask your Son
about tired?
I count on his intercession,
and I am packing it in.
Amen.

Closing

Day Nineteen

Presence | Living God,
if I'm to find my honest self by leaving myself behind,
then scour my heart of resentment.
It leeches on my time.

Grace | Abba, as I am ransomed, set me to ransom others.

Psalm | The Spirit of the Lord God has seized my soul,
and he has commissioned me to liberate the poor,
to bind the broken hearts of those who mourn,
to raise up the despondent and set the captives free,
to make an end of prisons, to cancel debts.
He bids me cry, "Today is the Amnesty of God!"

(Isaiah 61:1-2)

Hymn | At the round earth's imagined corners blow
Your trumpets, angels, and arise, arise
From death, you numberless infinities
Of souls, and to your scattered bodies go:
All whom the flood did, and fire shall o'erthrow,
All whom war, dearth, age, agues, tyrannies,
Despair, law, chance hath slain, and you whose eyes
Shall behold God, and never taste death's woe.
But let them sleep, Lord, and me mourn a space,
For if above all these my sins abound,
'Tis late to ask abundance of thy grace
When we are there. Here on this lowly ground
Teach me how to repent: for that's as good
As if thou hadst sealed my pardon with thy blood.

(John Donne)

112

God, my Friend,
this day is yours.
I offer you my acceptance
of whatever you send —
suffering, joy, toil, trouble —
ennobled far beyond my means
because it comes through the greatest gift
you gave me to offer,
Jesus, your Son, our Eucharist.
I pray not to change your mind,
only to understand it,
to yield to it.
But I do ask you to be with me,
especially in....
And I ask your loving watchfulness
for my friend....
Help me find you, through the day,
beneath all your surprising disguises.
Amen.

DAYTIME

Living God,
I trust you have patience with me.
You're perfect; I'm not.
So I trust you'll understand my difficulty
having patience with you.

Abba, light! Just give me light!

My God, my God, why have you abandoned me?
I call all day, all night. You are so silent!
I trust; you've rescued me and mine before.
Are they to say, "She trusted God. Well, look!"
You webbed me first within my mother's womb;
you drew me forth into the cold, the noise, the pain;
and yet each setback was an invitation to break out
once more, to reach for a greater, new horizon.
But now I see no new horizon, only darkness —
ahead, behind, within. Where is the light?
My soul is like water trickling through my fingers;

my bones have become unstrung, my heart like wax;
my mouth is dry as brick; my tongue licks dust.
They say, Great Friend, you dote on the poor in spirit.
Well, my soul feels poor as any mother's child's.

(Psalm 22)

Hymn | I wake and feel the fell of dark, not day.
What hours, O what black hours we have spent
This night! What sights you, heart, saw; ways you went!
And more must, in yet longer light's delay.
With witness I speak this. But where I say
Hours I mean years, mean life. And my lament
Is cries countless, cries like dead letters sent
To dearest him that lives alas! away.

I am gall, I am heartburn. God's most deep decree
Bitter would have me taste: my taste was me;
Bones built in me, flesh filled, blood brimmed the curse.
Selfyeast of spirit a dull dough sours. I see
The lost are like this, and their scourge to be
As I am mine, their sweating selves; but worse.

(Gerard Manley Hopkins)

Reading | Hence as suicide is the typical expression of the stoic spirit,
and battle of the warrior spirit, martyrdom always remains
the supreme enacting and perfection of Christianity. This
great action has been initiated for us, done on our behalf,
exemplified for our imitation, and inconceivably communi-
cated to all believers, by Christ on Calvary. There the degree
of accepted Death reaches the utmost bounds of the im-
aginable and perhaps goes beyond them; not only all natural
supports, but the presence of the very Father to whom the
sacrifice is made deserts the victim, and surrender to God
does not falter though God "forsakes" it.

(C.S. Lewis)

114

At noon, darkness fell on the land until midday. And at that time, Jesus screamed, "My God! My God! Why have you abandoned me?" Some of the spectators heard him and whispered, "The man's calling on Elijah." And one ran quickly to get a sponge, dipped it in cheap wine, and reached it up on a reed to slake Jesus' thirst. "No, no!" the rest shouted at him. "Leave him alone! Maybe Elijah will come, and we'll be here to see it!"

At that final moment, Jesus cried out in a loud voice and yielded his spirit to his Father.

(Matthew 27:45-50)

God, my Friend,
So. That's the answer then:
no shame in *feeling* deserted,
so long as I cling
to believing
I've not been.
I'll try.
Amen.

Living God,
paradoxes abound with you:
challenging and cherishing,
harrowing and hallowing,
lion and lamb.
Mother-Father,
right now, be more Mother to me, please.

Abba, like you, let me bring life out of death.

From the barren loins of Jesse springs a sprout!
And from those arid roots shall rise a kingdom.
The spirit of the Lord shall come to rest on him,
and from his mouth will come the breath of God.
He will not judge from surfaces or by vote.
He will give the wretched fairness,
the hopeless hope.
His word is a rod to strike the ruthless down.

The wolf will lie with the lamb in feral peace;
calves and lion cubs will feed together;
lions will share the cattle's straw and yet be lions.
The land will be as full of knowing God
   as seas are filled with water.

(Isaiah 11:1-9)

Hymn Most glorious Lord of life that on this day
Didst make Thy triumph over death and sin,
And having harrowed hell didst bring away
Captivity thence captive us to win;
This joyous day, dear Lord, with joy begin
And grant that we, for whom Thou didst die
Being with Thy dear blood clean washed from sin,
May live forever in felicity.

And that Thy love we weighing worthily,
May likewise love Thee for the same again;
And for Thy sake that all like dear didst buy,
With love may one another entertain.
So let us love, dear love, like as we ought,
Love is the lesson which the Lord us taught.

(Edmund Spenser)

Closing Holy Friend,
remind me once again
that love is not what I feel for them
but what I choose to do for them.
Amen.

Day Twenty

Living God,
so few of those around me
are people I chose —
my family, friends, neighbors.
Most of them just...happened.
Oh. I see.
You chose them for me.

Presence

Abba, to be useful, let me be used.

Grace

I saw Lord Yahweh sitting on a throne of light.
Above him seraphs hovered singing,
"Holy! Holy, holy, holy is the Lord of Hosts!"
The foundation trembled from the sound of their song,
and the temple filled with smoke and I cried in fear:
"What a wretch I am! I am doomed by my unclean lips!
And I live in a land with a people of unclean lips.
And yet my eyes have looked on the Lord of Hosts!"
Then one of the seraphs flew at me with a hot coal
pinched from the altar's fire in a pair of tongs.
The seraph pressed the ember to my lips and said,
"See! This pain has purged your lips of sin!"
And I heard the voice of the Lord thundering forth:
"Whom shall we send? Who will go for us?"
And I heard my own small voice say, "Here! Send me."
(Isaiah 6:1-9)

Psalm

Sail forth — steer for the deep waters only,
Reckless O Soul, exploring, I with thee,
   and thou with me,

Hymn

117

For we are bound where mariner has not yet dared to go,
And we will risk the ship, ourselves and all.

O my brave soul!
O farther, farther sail!
O daring joy, but safe!
  are they not all the seas of God?
O farther, farther, farther sail!

(Walt Whitman)

Offering | God, my Friend,
this day is yours.
I offer you my acceptance
of whatever you send —
suffering, joy, toil, trouble —
ennobled far beyond my means
because it comes through the greatest gift
you gave me to offer,
Jesus, your Son, our Eucharist.
I pray not to change your mind,
only to understand it,
to yield to it.
But I do ask you to be with me,
especially in....
And I ask your loving watchfulness
for my friend....
Help me find you, through the day,
beneath all your surprising disguises.
Amen.

DAYTIME

Presence | Living God,
there was a song: "I Can't Get No Satisfaction."
I wonder if the reason for that complaint
was that they were looking for joy
in the wrong place.

Grace | Abba, let my life be a light!

Have mercy, Lord, in your never-ending love.
Whatever wickedness I've done, trivial or terrible,
I've laid at your feet with honest heart.
Wash it white; turn it into wisdom.
You know all, and yet you will forget my faults,
because I am more important than my sins.
My sacrifice is my spirit, broken and renewed.
Give me a serene heart, genuine and truthful.
Help me pick from my pain the bits of light.
Break me out of the iron cage of suffering
so I can seed them into the days of those about me,
lessen the darkness, set ablaze the night.
Refined in this crucible, turn me into light!

(Psalm 51)

I cannot find my way: there is no star
In all the shrouded heavens anywhere;
And there is not a whisper in the air
Of any living voice but one so far
That I can hear it only as a bar
Of lost, imperial music, played when fair
And angel fingers wove, and unaware,
Dead leaves to garlands where no roses are.
No, there is not a glimmer, nor a call,
For one that welcomes, welcomes when he fears,
The black and awful chaos of the night;
But through it all, — above, beyond it all —
I know the far-sent message of the years,
I feel the coming glory of the Light!

(Edwin Arlington Robinson)

Faustus: Who made thee?
Mephistopheles: God; as the light makes the shadow.
Faustus: Is God, then, evil?
Mephistopheles: God is only light,
  And in the heart of the light no shadow standeth,
  Nor can I dwell within the light of heaven
  Where God is all.
Faustus: What art thou, Mephistopheles?

Mephistopheles: I am the price that all things pay for being,
The shadow on the world, thrown by the world
Standing in its own light, which light God is.

(Dorothy Sayers)

Scripture | Light enters the soul through the eyes. If your eyes are clear and receptive, your whole inner self is flooded with light and you see the wondrous treasure of life. But if your eyes are diseased by envy, bitterness, fear of the truth, how great the darkness within and without.

(Matthew 6:22-23)

Closing | God, my Friend,
let me be clear-eyed, honest.
Let me see what's truly there
and deal with that.
Amen.

EVENING

Presence | Living God,
I've never been too comfortable
with those who preach merely "Jesus-meek-and-mild."
It is as if the Lamb of God
had devoured
the Lion of Judah.

Grace | Abba, share your resolve with me.

Psalm | People who walked in the dark have seen a great light.
Out of a land of shadows, the dawn has arisen.
God, you make our gladness great; our joy takes wing!
You crack the yoke and rod that broke our shoulders.
The gear of war are shattered and in flames.
For unto us a child is born, a son is given!
And the cross shall be upon his shoulders.
And his names shall be shouted: "Wonderful!
Counselor! The mighty God! The everlasting Power!
The Prince of Peace!"

(Isaiah 9:1-6)

120

Glorious the northern lights astream;
Glorious the song, when God's the theme;
Glorious the thunder's roar:
Glorious hosanna from the den;
Glorious the catholic amen;
Glorious the martyr's gore:

Glorious — more glorious is the crown
Of him that brought salvation down
By meekness, called thy Son;
Thou that stupendous truth believed,
And now the matchless deed's achieved,
DETERMINED, DARED, and DONE.

(Christopher Smart)

Holy Friend,
my meekness is not mere defeated helplessness.
Help me, freely, to submit to your will,
embrace it as my own.
Amen.

Day Twenty-one

Presence Living God,
you send me messages all day —
rarely, I find, through Balaam's ass
(though those I find aplenty!).
Help me be attentive
to the cryptic voices you use
to bid me further.

Grace Abba, let me listen.

Psalm There seems to be a pattern in my life:
I trust in leaders, churchmen, lawyers, clerks.
And more than half the time they betray my trust.
Who are they, compounded of the same dust as I?
Oh, swathed up in brocade, to be sure.
  Armed with degrees.
Looking along the length of well-schooled noses.
Yet where are their hearts?
  Have they been schooled in pain?
Ah, then I would listen, sit me down at feet
that show the nail holes,
  the breast broached by a spear.

                                                                (Psalm 146)

Hymn O, a little talk wid Jesus makes it right;
Little talk wid Jesus makes it right, all right!
Lord, troubles of every kind,
Thank God, I'll always find
Dat a little talk wid Jesus makes it right.

My brother, I remember,
When I was a sinner lost,
I cried, "Have mercy, Jesus!"
But still my soul was toss'd,
Till I heard King Jesus say,
"Come here, I am de way,"
An' a little talk wid Jesus makes it right.

Sometimes de forked lightnin'
An' mutterin' thunder, too,
Of trials an' temptation
Make it hard for me an' you.
But Jesus is our fren'.
He'll keep us to de en',
An' a little talk wid Jesus makes it right.

(an unknown black poet)

Offering

God, my Friend,
this day is yours.
I offer you my acceptance
of whatever you send —
suffering, joy, toil, trouble —
ennobled far beyond my means
because it comes through the greatest gift
you gave me to offer,
Jesus, your Son, our Eucharist.
I pray not to change your mind,
only to understand it,
to yield to it.
But I do ask you to be with me,
especially in....
And I ask your loving watchfulness
for my friend....
Help me find you, through the day,
beneath all your surprising disguises.
Amen.

Presence | Living God,
in the past, dealing with you,
I used to shrug, quit, knuckle under, pout.
But since I've begun to wrestle with you —
though, of course, you always win —
I think we're better friends.

Grace | Abba, wedge my heart open, and ready.

Psalm | Open-hearted sufferers are in the hands of God.
They seem, in the eyes of the foolish, as good as dead,
their lives an annihilation, yet they are at peace.
The shortsighted see such lives as cursed, and yet
their hope is the seed of everlasting life.
Chastened awhile, like ore in a crucible of fire,
they emerge more precious than the purest gold.
The wounds are decorations, badges of fire.
When Yahweh comes,
they will dart like sparks through stubble
and set the world ablaze!
Those who trust in God
will know the truth:
that the faithful live in love,
that those worthy of the gift of trial will triumph!

(Wisdom 3:1-9)

Hymn | Come, O thou Traveller unknown,
  Whom still I hold, but cannot see,
My company before is gone,
  And I am left alone with thee,
With thee all night I mean to stay,
And wrestle till the break of day.

I need not tell thee who I am,
  My misery, or sin declare,
Thyself hast called me by my name,
  Look on thy hands, and read it there,
But who, I ask thee, who art thou?
Tell me thy name, and tell me now.

124

In vain thou strugglest to get free,
　I never will unloose my hold:
Art thou the Man that died for me?
　The secret of thy love unfold.
Wrestling I will not let thee go,
Till I thy name, thy nature know....

Contented now upon my thigh
　I halt, till life's short journey end;
All helplessness, all weakness I,
　On thee alone for strength depend,
Nor have I power, from thee, to move;
Thy nature and thy name is Love.

Lame as I am, I take the prey,
　Hell, earth, and sin with ease o'ercome;
I leap for joy, pursue my way,
　And as a bounding hart fly home,
Through all eternity to prove
Thy nature and thy name is Love.

(Charles Wesley)

Reading

The way in which a man accepts his fate and all the suffering it entails, the way in which he takes up his cross, gives him ample opportunity — even under the most difficult circumstances — to add a deeper meaning to his life. It may remain brave, dignified and unselfish. Or in the bitter fight for self-preservation he may forget his human dignity and become no more than an animal. Here lies the chance for a man either to make use of or to forego the opportunities of attaining the moral values that a difficult situation may afford him. And this decides whether he is worthy of his sufferings or not.

(Victor Frankl)

Scripture	The full Senate of Israel agreed with Gamaliel's advice. So they summoned the apostles and gave orders for them to be flogged. Then they warned them never to speak in the name of Jesus again, and they released them. The apostles left the presence of the Sanhedrin, bursting with joy! Because God had considered them worthy enough to suffer in the name of Jesus. And day after day, they continued to preach that name. (Acts of the Apostles 5:40-42)
Closing	God, my Friend, if you send me setbacks, let me be proud that you trust me enough to offer them to me. Amen.

EVENING

Presence	Living God, there is a grudge festering in the darker places of my soul. You know which one it is, far better than I. Oh, we never mention it. We're civil. We get on with things. Lord, lance that grudge! Make me swallow my bruised feelings and make peace.
Grace	Abba, make me a place where forgiveness happens.
Psalm	The test of honest love is patient kindness. Love never frets that the beloved loves others, too. Love never sneers or belittles or boasts. It is never rude or grasping or self-absorbed. Love is not thin-skinned or quick to take offense. It holds no grudges but forgives and honestly forgets. Love does not make little lists of others' faults; it does not deal in rumors but delights in truth. Love is ever ready to excuse, to trust, to hope, to endure whatever comes. (1 Corinthians 13:4-7)

Love is not all: it is not meat nor drink
Nor slumber nor a roof against the rain;
Nor yet a floating spar to men that sink
And rise and sink and rise and sink again;
Love cannot fill the thickened lung with breath,
Nor clean the blood, nor set the fractured bone;
Yet many a man is making friends with death
Even as I speak, for lack of love alone.
It well may be that in a difficult hour,
Pinned down by pain and moaning for release,
Or nagged by want past resolution's power,
I might be driven to sell your love for peace,
Or trade the memory of this night for food.
It well may be. I do not think I would.

(Edna St. Vincent Millay)

Hymn

Holy Friend,
tomorrow, I promise,
I will open that grudge and heal it.
If forgiveness is not forthcoming,
at least I'll have tried.
Amen.

Closing

Day Twenty-two

Presence | Living God,
if I honestly trusted
that whatever comes,
comes from you,
why don't I welcome setbacks
as challenges?

Grace | Abba, uproot all fear from me.

Psalm | Love will come to perfection in us only
when we can face the Day of Judgment without fear,
because we have become as docile to God as Jesus.
Love of God can't live with fear of God.
Love can never share a soul with fear,
for fear is dispossessed by genuine love.
To fear, you see, is to be looking for punishment,
and why would lover or beloved punish one another?
To be afraid, then, is not to know what loving means.
We must love because we know God loved us first,
which ennobles us to be worthy to be loved and love.
Anyone who says "I love God" yet hates is a liar.
Those who cannot love the people they see
surely cannot love the God they have never seen.
Our claim to love God is our claim to love one another.

(1 John 4:17-21)

Hymn | Oh, yet we trust that somehow good
Will be the final goal of ill,
To pangs of nature, sins of will,
Defects of doubt, and taints of blood;

That nothing walks with aimless feet;
That not one life shall be destroyed,
Or cast as rubbish to the void,
When God hath made the pile complete....

Behold, we know not anything;
I can but trust that good shall fall
At last — far off — at last, to all,
And every winter change to spring.

So runs my dream: but what am I?
An infant crying in the night:
An infant crying for the light:
And with no language but a cry.

                              (Alfred, Lord Tennyson)

God, my Friend,   **Offering**
this day is yours.
I offer you my acceptance
of whatever you send —
suffering, joy, toil, trouble —
ennobled far beyond my means
because it comes through the greatest gift
you gave me to offer,
Jesus, your Son, our Eucharist.
I pray not to change your mind,
only to understand it,
to yield to it.
But I do ask you to be with me,
especially in....
And I ask your loving watchfulness
for my friend....
Help me find you, through the day,
beneath all your surprising disguises.
Amen.

DAYTIME

Presence | Living God,
I wonder if you understand time,
not the concept, but the *feel* of it,
how it drags,
how it tyrannizes,
how it slips irretrievably away.

Grace | Abba, make me grateful to be alive.

Psalm | Lord, my life seems to ebb away like candle smoke.
My bones smolder within my fevered skin.
Food is ashes. I groan aloud, alone.
My soul soars the barrens like a shattered hawk;
like an old screech owl, it squawks among the ruins.
Did you pick me up only to throw me aside
like a child no longer smitten with a toy?
Oh, Lord, cut me not off in the midst of my days.
You wear the heavens you made like a silken garment
that will one day wear thin and be cast away,
but you yourself will never change or cease.
Let me trust that somewhere within my fragile self
there is a spark of your unextinguishable life,
that my pain is less negligible than the heavens.

(Psalm 102)

Hymn | Vital spark of heavenly flame!
Quit, O quit this mortal frame:
Trembling, hoping, lingering, flying,
O the pain, the bliss of dying!
Cease, fond Nature, cease thy strife,
And let me languish into life.

Hark! they whisper; angels say,
Sister Spirit, come away!
What is this absorbs me quite?
Steals my senses, shuts my sight,
Drowns my spirits, draws my breath?
Tell me, my soul, can this be Death?

130

The world recedes; it disappears!
Heav'n opens on my eyes! my ears
With sounds seraphic ring.

Lend, lend your wings! I mount! I fly!
O Grave! where is thy victory?
O Death! where is thy sting?

(Alexander Pope)

Reading

Life has always seemed to me like a plant that lives on its rhizome. Its true life is invisible, hidden in the rhizome. The part that appears above ground lasts only a single summer. Then it withers away — an ephemeral apparition. When we think of the unending growth and decay of life and civilization, we cannot escape the impression of absolute nullity. Yet I have never lost a sense of something that lives and endures underneath the eternal flux. What we see is the blossom, which passes. The rhizome remains.

(C.J. Jung)

Scripture

I'm telling you this in the strongest words I know: Unless a grain of wheat is consumed by the earth and dies, it remains only a single lifeless grain — unfulfilled potential. But if it submits to suffering and death, ah! What a harvest of life! If you dote on your life, you destroy your life. If you sacrifice your life for me in this life, you will keep your soul unto forever.

(John 12:24-25)

Closing

God, my Friend,
I surely don't crave suffering.
But if you send it,
make me more creative
than I've been.
Amen.

EVENING

Presence

Living God,
I begin to believe
that sin means more to us than it does to you,

131

that you are far more concerned
with lives left unfulfilled.

Grace | Abba, let me live worthy of Christ's ransom.

Psalm | Our faith in Christ Jesus brings us to peace with God,
calls us into grace, so we boast that we await God's glory!
But more, we can boast that God trusts us to suffer.
And enduring pain is the only path to patience,
and patience brings perseverance and her sister, hope.
That hope is not deceptive; it is sealed by the Spirit
who ransomed us at the price of the blood of Christ.
Christ died because we were helpless to save ourselves.
One truly brave, perhaps, could die for someone good,
but what proves God's undying love for us
is that Christ died for us *despite* our sins!
Is it likely that, having died to make us worthy,
Christ would fail to see us through these trials?
Having saved us once, would he fail to save us again?
Let us rejoice, not only that Christ has made our peace
but that he is the rock in whom we root our trust.

(Romans 5:1-11)

Hymn | Tell me not, in mournful numbers
Life is but an empty dream!
For the soul is dead that slumbers,
And things are not what they seem.

Life is real! Life is earnest!
And the grave is not its goal;
"Dust thou art, to dust returnest,"
Was not spoken of the soul.

(Henry Wadsworth Longfellow)

Closing | Holy Friend,
today was a gift
which I now return,
at least slightly improved, I hope,
and gladly await
the next.
Amen.

Day Twenty-three

Living God,
occasionally (not *too* often)
remind me
that this life is only
a temporary assignment.

Presence

Abba, make me enjoy what I have while I have it.

Grace

If only you'd stop worrying about yourselves!
"What are we to eat? My body is so contemptible!
They laugh at my clothes!" Life means more than food!
The body is more precious than what you wrap it in!
Look up at the crows. They neither sow nor reap.
Their days are not fraught with building bigger barns.
Yet God provides that, somehow, they survive.
For all your fretting, can you add a day to your life?
One tick of time is out of your hands, so let it go!
Look at the flowers. No spinners or weavers there.
Yet Solomon's splendor pales compared to them.
If God arrays mere weeds with such solicitude,
with what exquisite concern must God be watching you!
You have such little faith! God sees. God knows.

(Luke 12:22-30)

Psalm

Fear no more the heat of the sun,
Nor the furious winter's rages;
Thou thy worldly task hast done,
Home art gone, and ta'en thy wages.
Golden lads and girls all must,
As chimney-sweepers, come to dust.

Hymn

Fear no more the frown o' the great;
Thou art past the tyrant's stroke.
Care no more to clothe and eat;
To thee the reed is as the oak.
The sceptre, learning, physic, must
All follow this, and come to dust.

Fear no more the lightning flash,
Nor the all-dreaded thunder-stone;
Fear not slander, censure rash;
Thou hast finished joy and moan.
All lovers young, all lovers must
Consign to thee and come to dust.

(William Shakespeare)

Offering

God, my Friend,
this day is yours.
I offer you my acceptance
of whatever you send —
suffering, joy, toil, trouble —
ennobled far beyond my means
because it comes through the greatest gift
you gave me to offer,
Jesus, your Son, our Eucharist.
I pray not to change your mind,
only to understand it,
to yield to it.
But I do ask you to be with me,
especially in….
And I ask your loving watchfulness
for my friend….
Help me find you, through the day,
beneath all your surprising disguises.
Amen.

DAYTIME

Presence

Living God,
I know my place before you:
neither your equal
nor negligible.

134

You made me a Peer of the Realm,
so, if I sometimes offer you advice,
feel free to act otherwise.

Abba, don't let me confuse my weakness with your wrath.　　**Grace**

Great God,　　**Psalm**
you are not a Lord of rage, revenge, rebuke.
Pity me. My nerves are stripped and raw.
My aching bones torment me, and I'm weary.
My very soul is shriveled, like a rag.
How long, O Lord, how long? How long?
How long will you be? I grow impatient, Lord.

Listen to me! *I* grow impatient with *you!*
The pot rebuking the potter,
the poem chastising the poet,
the mirror reflecting itself.

To speak the truth, Great Friend, I weary of tears.
This enemy within me gnaws my soul and makes me old.
Perhaps my sighs bespeak some sort of praise,
better perhaps than the silence of the grave.
I trust you hear my tears, my praise, my prayer.

(Psalm 6)

Love is swift of foot,　　**Hymn**
Love's a man of war,
　　And can shoot,
And can hit from far.

Who can 'scape his bow?
That which wrought on thee,
　　Brought thee low,
Needs must work on me.

Throw away thy rod:
Though man frailties hath,
　　Thou art God:
Throw away thy wrath.

(George Herbert)

Reading | You asked for a loving God: you have one. The great spirit you so lightly invoked, the "lord of terrible aspect" is present: not a senile benevolence that drowsily wishes you to be happy in your own way, not the cold philanthropy of a conscientious magistrate, nor the care of a host who feels responsible for the comfort of his guests, but the consuming fire Himself, the Love that made the worlds, persistent as the artist's love for his work and despotic as a man's love for a dog, provident and venerable as a father's love for a child, jealous, inexorable, exacting as love between the sexes.

(C.S. Lewis)

Scripture | Then from the core of the whirlwind, Yahweh gave Job his answer: "Who is this who carps at my plans with his dull-witted words? Brace yourself, battler. It's my turn. Where were you when I laid the foundations of the earth? Tell me, if you are so perceptive. Who decided the earth's dimensions, eh? Or stretched the measuring tape around it? Do you know what supports it in the darkness? Who set it spinning in that dawn of dawns when all the stars were singing for joy and all angels of God were chanting praise? Speak!"

(Job 38:2-7)

Closing | God, my Friend,
when I think you're a pushover,
stand me before the stars.
When I think you're a tyrant,
show me a child asleep.
Amen.

EVENING

Presence | Living God,
unless I am willing
to be taken in,
I will never know
the heart of anything.

Grace | Abba, scuttle my quest for certitudes.

Lord, I am not vain (I tell myself).   **Psalm**
No danger of arrogance with me (I swear on my knees).
I don't trouble myself with matters of moment (but me).
I avoid thorny problems (except "Am I doing it right?")
My soul is tranquil, silent (they're watching, I know!)
as a dozing child on its mother's lap (what's wrong?),
content to be weaned (I'm here adrift and alone!).
I hope in God forever. (No guarantee?)

Gracious Friend, there must be an end of my diddling.
There must be a time when I let go the crag and leap!
All right, now! All right, now! Yes, I will!
    Just you wait! Here I come!
Or maybe it's wiser to wait. Not right now.

                                               (Psalm 131)

My thoughtless youth was winged with vain desires,   **Hymn**
My manhood, long misled by wandering fires,
Followed false lights; and when their glimpse was gone
My pride struck out new sparkles of her own.
Such was I, such by nature still I am;
Be Thine the glory, and be mine the shame!
Good life be now my task: my doubts are done;
(What more could fright my faith than Three in One?)
                                            (John Dryden)

Holy Friend,   **Closing**
now I shut down the engines
of my quizzical mind
and rest serene
with you.
Amen.

Day Twenty-four

Presence Living God,
Isaiah dwelt among a people of unclean lips.
And so do I.
But what troubles me far more
is their narrowed minds,
their hardened hearts.

Grace Abba, make me just a touch more gullible.

Psalm "God sees nothing," the sophisticated say.
"If he even exists, he surely has better things to do."

Did some doddering blind woman fashion the eye?
Is the One who invented the ear unable to hear?
The first step toward wisdom is a humble heart,
and if that be true, let me be proud to be humble,
willing to follow the Truth, wherever she leads.
I am blessed to be instructed in the ways
   of the human mind
by the One who was truth before the mind was made.
I have only to cry, "I am overwhelmed by doubt!"
and the Lord of Truth will ease my panicky soul,
not giving me answers, but being my answer.

(Psalm 94)

Hymn Margaret, are you grieving
Over Goldengrove unleaving?
Leaves, like the things of man, you
With your fresh thoughts care for, can you?
Ah! As the heart grows older

It will come to such sights colder
By and by, nor spare a sigh
Though worlds of wanwood leafmeal lie;
And yet you will weep and know why.

Now no matter, child, the name:
Sorrow's springs are the same.
Nor mouth had, no nor mind, expressed
What heart heard of, ghost guessed:
It is the blight man was born for,
It is Margaret you mourn for.

(Gerard Manley Hopkins)

God, my Friend,
this day is yours.
I offer you my acceptance
of whatever you send —
suffering, joy, toil, trouble —
ennobled far beyond my means
because it comes through the greatest gift
you gave me to offer,
Jesus, your Son, our Eucharist.
I pray not to change your mind,
only to understand it,
to yield to it.
But I do ask you to be with me,
especially in....
And I ask your loving watchfulness
for my friend....
Help me find you, through the day,
beneath all your surprising disguises.
Amen.

Offering

DAYTIME

Living God,
I don't know why
it keeps surprising me
that I can always endure more
than I thought possible.

Presence

139

Grace	Abba, let me take honest pride in my scars.
Psalm	God, I lift my soul to you, as in a cup.
	It is all I have to offer, and thus enough,
	since, had I more, it would be yours as well.
	With nothing left, I must rely on you.
	And so I do.
	Remember not my sins or my regrets
	But only your infinite eagerness to forgive.
	I will praise your loving kindness every day I live.
	And so I do.
	If it be your will, release me from this net
	of pain that frightens me, so I may live.
	If not, I place that in the cup I offer, too.
	And so I do.
	(Psalm 25)
Hymn	And the wild regrets, and the bloody sweats,
	None knew so well as I:
	For he who lives more lives than one
	More deaths than one must die....
	I know not whether Laws be right,
	Or whether Laws be wrong;
	All that we know who lie in gaol
	Is that the wall is strong;
	And that each day is like a year,
	A year whose days are long....
	How else but through a broken heart
	May Lord Christ enter in?
	(Oscar Wilde)
Reading	A more essential condition is the willingness to be devastated, by which I mean the willingness to let the mortal wounds penetrate one's heart so deeply that it is broken completely open by it. This is, I think, a pregnant image. For it suggests that the deepest lessons the heart has to deliver to us become accessible only when it is ruptured. It is anguish that makes the heart an open book because the wound it causes pierces all the way through to its core. These are terrible lessons, the kind that fill one with nausea. We like to think our lives would be happier if we could find a way to

140

avoid learning them; but the only way to do that is to close one's heart and keep it closed, so that nothing gets in or out of it — to make oneself a heart of stone. It is terrible to put into words the one real alternative to this avoidance. But I see no way to get around what seems to be the harshest, the most merciless truth about the human heart — I mean the fact that, to keep it open, once it has been pierced, one must allow it to be an open wound.

(Jerome Miller)

On the night he was betrayed, the Lord Jesus took bread, blessed and broke it, and said, "This is my body, which will be broken for you. In my memory, you do the same." After supper, he took a cup of wine and said, "This is the cup of the new covenant, sealed in my own blood. In my memory, you do the same. Until I return, every time you eat this bread and drink this cup, your sacrifice becomes one with mine."

(1 Corinthians 11:23-27)

Scripture

God, my Friend,
let me understand that — to live —
I must break myself up, or be broken,
to share the pieces.
Amen.

Closing

EVENING

Living God,
if by some miracle
I could have more confidence in you,
I'd have fewer doubts about myself.
I'm in the market
for such a miracle.

Presence

Abba, make us as smitten with you as you are with us.

Grace

It is the Lord God Yahweh who speaks:
"I ignite a million million suns in the night.
I rile the waves of the sea till the waters roar.
And every species but yours obeys my will.
Yet if — and only if — by some impossible chance,

Psalm

the rest of my creation joined with you,
betrayed my trust and scorned my plans,
if the planets stopped in their tracks
   and refused to spin,
if deserts bloomed,
   and rivers flowed uphill,
if doves turned savage,
   and lions beat their breasts,
then — and only then — would I forget you."

(Jeremiah 31:35-37)

Hymn | when serpents bargain for the right to squirm
and the sun strikes to gain a living wage —
when thorns regard their roses with alarm
and rainbows are insured against old age

when every thrush may sing no new moon in
if all screech-owls have not okayed his voice
— and any wave signs on the dotted line
or else an ocean is compelled to close

when the oak begs permission of the birch
to make an acorn — valleys accuse their
mountains of having altitude — and march
denounces april as a saboteur

then we'll believe in that incredible
unanimal mankind(and not until)

(e.e. cummings)

Closing | Holy Friend,
the fact you dote on
someone like me
is too good to be true.
Help me yield my self-doubting defenses
to the joy of knowing
that it is.
Amen.

Day Twenty-five

Living God,
it is an intimidating honor
to be invited into the Trinity family.
Let me always be aware of that.

Presence

Abba, remind me that this life is a warmup.

Grace

God never said to an angel, "You are my Son!"
No, when God sent his firstborn among us,
God sent the angels as heralds of flame on the wind,
to minister to him, to guard his ways, to worship.
But about the Son, God said, "Your Kingdom is forever.
The one rule of your Realm will be an honest heart.
You will welcome the honorable and true
    and disown the devious.
The heavens we created will disappear,
    but you will remain.
We will fold them like a worn-out coat,
    but you will live forever.
God never said to an angel, "You are my Son!"
But, my sons and daughters, God says that to you.
                                    (Hebrews 1:5-13)

Psalm

It must be so — Plato, thou reason'st well —
Else whence this pleasing hope, this fond desire,
This longing after immortality?
Or whence this secret dread, and inward horror,
Of falling into naught? Why shrinks the soul
Back on herself, and startles at destruction?
'Tis the divinity that stirs within us;

Hymn

'Tis heaven itself, that points out an hereafter,
And intimates eternity to man.
Eternity! thou pleasing, dreadful thought!

(Joseph Addison)

Offering

God, my Friend,
this day is yours.
I offer you my acceptance
of whatever you send —
suffering, joy, toil, trouble —
ennobled far beyond my means
because it comes through the greatest gift
you gave me to offer,
Jesus, your Son, our Eucharist.
I pray not to change your mind,
only to understand it,
to yield to it.
But I do ask you to be with me,
especially in....
And I ask your loving watchfulness
for my friend....
Help me find you, through the day,
beneath all your surprising disguises.
Amen.

DAYTIME

Presence

Living God,
channel my resentment
into a challenge,
into creating a newer life,
one that's contagious.

Grace

Abba, convince me joy is worth any cost.

Psalm

Enough of anger. Set rage aside and live.
Why waste the time I have with worry over
what only God can know? The road leads on.
Whether to light or further darkness no one
can predict. The enemy within will win —
or I will win. Till then, the enemy is friend,

144

goading me toward God, to give in to God,
which gives a purpose to my days: defiance.
I will *not* surrender while God is at my side.
Till then, each day I don't relent becomes
another weapon, salvaged from the sea.

(Psalm 37)

Hymn

I was ever a fighter, so — one fight more,
    The best and the last!
I would hate that death bandaged my eyes, and forbore,
    And bade me creep past.
No! let me taste the whole of it, fare like my peers
    The heroes of old,
Bear the brunt, in a minute pay glad life's arrears
    Of pain, darkness and cold.
For sudden the worst turns the best to the brave,
    The black minute's at end,
And the elements' rage, the fiend-voices that rave,
    Shall dwindle, shall blend,
Shall change, shall become first a peace out of pain,
    Then a light, then thy breast,
O thou soul of my soul! I shall clasp thee again,
    And with God be the rest!

(Robert Browning)

Reading

When my patients lose sight of their significance and are disheartened by the effort of the work we are doing, I sometimes tell them that the human race is in the midst of making an evolutionary leap. "Whether or not we succeed in that leap," I say to them, "is your personal responsibility." And mine. The universe, this stepping-stone, has been laid down to prepare a way for us. But we ourselves must step across it, one by one. Through grace we are helped not to stumble and through grace we know that *we are* being welcomed. What more can we ask?

(M. Scott Peck)

Scripture

My friends, look at our lives this way: flesh and blood cannot march into the kingdom of God; the perishable cannot live in a reality in which nothing perishes. Here is our great secret: the imperishable in us can never truly die! We shall be

145

changed, marvelously, instantaneously, in the twinkling of
an eye! Everything imperishable in us will be raised. For now,
it is our task to change anything in our hearts which is
perishable into what can live into eternal life....So never give
in, my friends. Never admit defeat. Keep always busy with
your work for the Lord, because you know that — no matter
what — your struggle is never in vain.

(1 Corinthians 15:50-53, 58)

Closing | God, my Friend,
purge me of all that is petty,
puritanical, peevish, pinched-hearted.
Give me the susceptibility
Jesus always had.
Amen.

EVENING

Presence | Living God,
tragically, we Christians bicker
among ourselves about such trivia.
Make us comprehend and own
that Christ is so much more important
than critiques.

Grace | Abba, finding and forgiving is all I'm for.

Psalm | I am the good shepherd. I know mine. Mine know me.
I am ready to pay my life in ransom for my sheep.
Oh, there are other sheep
    you would not share pasture with.
They are mine as well, and I'll die for them as well.
In the end, they will hear my whistle and know it's me,
And then there will be just one flock, one Shepherd.
My Father loves me, for I love my sheep to the death.
No one steals my life; I give it freely.
And at my Father's will, I will take it up again.
As I have done, so, too, must you.

(John 10:14-18)

He's the Lily of the valley,
  He's mah Lawd;
He's the white Rose of Sharon,
  He's mah Lawd.

He's the Great Physician,
  He's mah Lawd;
He heals yo' sorrows,
  He's mah Lawd.

He's the Alpha and Omega, the beginning and the end,
  He's mah Lawd;
He's the Shepherd of the flock, the door to enter in,
  He's mah Lawd.

He's the Lord that was an' is to come,
  He's mah Lawd;
He's the Rock the church is built upon,
  He's mah Lawd.

He's the Bread of Heaven, the Truth, the Way,
  He's mah Lawd;
He's the Light that shines to a perfect day,
  He's mah Lawd.

I'll tell the nations, both great an' small,
  He's mah Lawd;
The blood of Jesus saves us all,
  He's mah Lawd.

                    (an unknown black poet)

Holy Friend,
all those titles are true.
That such a one
knows my name, calls me friend,
overwhelms me, and yet
without a whisper of fear.
Amen.

Day Twenty-six

Presence

Living God,
I search for you,
and you search for me.
Perhaps if I just stand still....

Grace

Abba, make me unafraid to be found.

Psalm

Out in the desolate, wind-worn wilderness God went,
the relentlessly patient Father of runaway souls.
Fearful of his wrath, I huddled from the howling wind
under a crop of rock, hoping he'd pass me by.
But he stopped, his shadow shielding me
    from the searing sand.
"Ah!" he said with a weary smile. "There you are."
And he stooped and pulled me
    into his strong, sheltering arms
and rocked me like a frightened, whimpering child.
"There, there," he whispered. "It's all right now.
    You're home."
And, as in a dream, he bore me up, above the storm,
into the cool sweet air, safe on his wings!

(Deuteronomy 32:10-11)

Hymn

I stood outside the gate;
They would not let me in — me in.
I prayed to my good Lawd,
To cleanse me from all sin — all sin.

Lord Jesus Christ, I seek to find,
Pray tell me whar He dwells — He dwells.

Oh, you go down in yonder fold
An' search among the sheep — the sheep.

There you will find Him, I am told
He's whar He loves to be — to be.
An' if I find Him how'll I know
Round any other man — other man?

He has Salvation awn His brow,
He has a wounded hand — wounded han'.
I thank you faw yo' advice —
I'll find Him ef I can — ef I can.

(an unknown black poet)

God, my Friend,
this day is yours.
I offer you my acceptance
of whatever you send —
suffering, joy, toil, trouble —
ennobled far beyond my means
because it comes through the greatest gift
you gave me to offer,
Jesus, your Son, our Eucharist.
I pray not to change your mind,
only to understand it,
to yield to it.
But I do ask you to be with me,
especially in....
And I ask your loving watchfulness
for my friend....
Help me find you, through the day,
beneath all your surprising disguises.
Amen.

DAYTIME

Offering

Presence

Living God,
each day seems a forever —
and yet is gone like a shot.
The problem is not with my clock
but with my mind.

Grace	Abba, take off my this-world blinders.
Psalm	O God, my God, you are from eternity to forever!
	Before mountains bellied up or earth was born,
	you are — without beginning, without end.
	To you, a thousand times ten thousand years
	are a flicker of an eye, a slight distraction.
	Through the tiny scope with which I view my life,
	the anxious days stretch inexorably ahead —
	"Tomorrow, and tomorrow and tomorrow, creeps
	in this petty pace...."
	Yet from the inaccessible light in which you dwell,
	my seventy years or so are the wake of a ship,
	a finger snapped, a whisper in a whirlwind.
	Lend me your eyes, and let me see my life
	as a privileged treasure of momentary gifts,
	too fleeting to cling to, too perishable to waste.
	But let me see my suffering as you do, too,
	an instant's shadow against an infinite light!

(Psalm 90)

Hymn	Free at las', free at las'!
	I thank God I'm free at las'!
	Free at las', free at las'!
	I thank God I'm free at las'!
	Way down yonder in de graveyard walk,
	I thank God I'm free at las'.
	Me an' my Jesus gwinter meet an' talk,
	I thank God I'm free at las'!
	On-a my knees when de light pass by,
	I thank God I'm free at las'.
	Tho't my soul would-a rise an' fly.
	I thank God I'm free at las'!
	Some o'dese mawnin's, bright an' fair,
	I thank God I'm free at las'.
	Gwine-ter meet my Jesus in de middle of de air.
	Thank God, I'm free at las'!

(an unknown black poet)

150

Already the only constant idea is that there exists something infinitely more just and happier than myself, it entirely fills me with immeasurable tenderness and glory, oh, whoever I am, whatever I have done. For man, a good deal more indispensable than his own happiness is to know and in every moment to believe that there exists in a certain place a perfect and calm happiness for everyone and for everything....The entire law of human existence consists solely in this: that man can always bow his head before that which is infinitely great. If human beings were deprived of that which is infinitely great, then they would not be able to live any longer and would die as victims of desperation.

(Fyodor Dostoyevsky)

All the things I used to think made me important I now see as silly — in fact, actual disadvantages. No value on earth can outweigh knowing Christ Jesus my Lord. For him, I can accept the loss of everything, as just so much trash compared to having a place within Christ. I no longer scrabble to save myself by my own efforts, trying to justify myself by assuring myself I've broken no laws. I want only the fulfillment that comes from God through Jesus Christ. All I need is the power of Christ's resurrection, and therefore, each day, I must share in his sufferings and death. Oh, I haven't won yet. But I'm still running!"

(Philippians 3:7-12)

God, my Friend,
help me see the difference
between "seems"
and "is."
Amen.

Living God,
in this play we're improvising,
I have a quite minor role —
merely a walk-on, in fact.
But help me play it well.

Grace	Abba, let me serve and not hanker for praise.
Psalm	Oh, no! I am not the bridegroom, just his friend. I stand and listen, ready when the bridegroom calls. I ask no more, as long as I am ready. He is the one who is important, you see, not I. He is above me, above all others born of seed. He comes with the secrets of heaven in his hands. Most won't listen; that can't change his truth, for the will of God is not ascertained by vote. Anyone who believes in the Son will never die. Those who scorn him don't know what living means. <div align="right">(John 3:29-35)</div>

Hymn	When fishes flew and forests walked
	    And figs grew upon thorn,
	Some moment when the moon was blood
	    Then surely I was born.
	
	With monstrous head and sickening cry
	    And ears like errant wings,
	The devils's walking parody
	    On all four-footed things.
	
	The tattered outlaw of the earth,
	    Of ancient crooked will;
	Starve, scourge, deride me: I am dumb,
	    I keep my secret still.
	
	Fools! For I also had my hour;
	    One far fierce hour and sweet:
	There was a shout about my ears,
	    And palms before my feet.
	<div align="right">(Gilbert K. Chesterton)</div>

Closing	Holy Friend, I'm happy to lay down our common burden for a while and sleep. Amen.

Day Twenty-seven

Living God,
there is a grandeur
in the commonplace
that I rarely take time to see.
Help me to comprehend
the glory at my elbows.

Presence

Abba, remind me heaven starts now.

Grace

Before "beginning" was, God expressed himself,
and that Word was with God, that Word was God.
The Word was with God before beginning began.
Among them, all that began was begun.
Not a thing enlivened with "is" began without them,
for the "is" in all that is is the life of God.
They are the light the darkness can't comprehend....
The true light, the Word, was coming among us,
entering the world that they themselves had made.
The Word came into the world and we scoffed at him.
But the few who saw through surfaces, he gifted:
he invited them into the Family of God,
and all reborn of him are enlivened by God.
The Word fused with flesh and dwelled among us,
and the life of God enlivens us even now.

(John 1:1-5, 9-14)

Psalm

Mine eyes have seen the glory
   of the coming of the Lord;
He is trampling out the vintage
   where the grapes of wrath are stored;

Hymn

153

He hath loosed the fateful lightning
   of His terrible swift sword;
His truth is marching on!

I have seen Him in the watchfires
   of a hundred circling camps;
They have builded Him an altar
   in the evening dews and damps;
I can read His righteous sentence
   by the dim and flaring lamps:
His day is marching on.

In the beauty of the lilies
   Christ was born across the sea,
With a glory in his bosom
   that transfigures you and me;
As He died to make men holy,
   let us live to make men free,
While God is marching on.

                            (Julia Ward Howe)

Offering | God, my Friend,
this day is yours.
I offer you my acceptance
of whatever you send —
suffering, joy, toil, trouble —
ennobled far beyond my means
because it comes through the greatest gift
you gave me to offer,
Jesus, your Son, our Eucharist.
I pray not to change your mind,
only to understand it,
to yield to it.
But I do ask you to be with me,
especially in....
And I ask your loving watchfulness
for my friend....
Help me find you, through the day,
beneath all your surprising disguises.
Amen.

Living God,
every little death
can be a new beginning.
Help me be unafraid
of new beginnings.

Abba, let me face time with an eye on forever.

Here, Yahweh will remove the mourning veil,
the shroud of sadness smothering all our lives.
He will destroy death for ever, and ever, and ever.
God will wipe the tears from every cheek,
and shame shall never more exist. God speaks!
That day we will say, "See! This is our God!
Yahweh, the only God in whom we hoped.
We exult that at last he has fulfilled his promise.
There will never more be pain. Or hopelessness.
   Or death."
                                        (Isaiah 25:7-12)

Someone asked,
"Do you have a book called 'My Divine Friend?' "

Not for me that book
Not for you that name.
Friend: A honey of a word, yes
gathered day by day, grain by grain
in a perennial rose garden
alive with laborious bees.
A good word, as it goes
of familiar ease but sticky
with a mildness alien to you.

You are not my friend, your love
is not decanted drop by slow drop
in tumblers and bottles.
You are the passion of the tempest
ever moving to the east and to the west
to the north and to the south.

You are the typhoon battering my house
blasting the door out of its hinges
flinging about the small treasures
assembled on tables and shelves.
You are dangerous, unpredictable,
a fiery breath burning me raw
pressing its brand upon my heart.
Who would believe what happened in the dark?
How the wind cracked my house
tore its walls asunder, blowing
time away, space away
until nothing was left
— only emptiness, nakedness, silence
and your seal upon my life
hotter than flame, brighter than light.

(Catherine deVinck)

Reading | They shall awake as Jacob did, and say as Jacob said, Surely the Lord is in this place, and this is no other but the house of God, and the gate of heaven, and into that gate they shall enter, and in that house they shall dwell, where there shall be no Cloud nor Sun, no darkness nor dazzling, but one equal light, no noise nor silence, but one equal music, no fears nor hopes, but one equal possession, no foes nor friends, but one equal communion and Identity, no ends nor beginnings, but one equal eternity.

(John Donne)

Scripture | Out of his endless glory, may God give you the power through his Spirit for your hidden self to keep growing so that, because of your faith, Christ will dwell in your hearts. Then, rooted and grounded in love, you will with all the saints be empowered to grasp the length and breadth, the height and depth, knowing the love of Christ which beggars understand. You will be filled with the utter fullness of God.

(Ephesians 3:16-19)

God, my Friend,
I am a very tiny tabernacle
to contain such bottomless love,
much less grasp it.
And yet a manger
was enough.
Amen.

Living God,
nothing outside me
can validate my soul,
except you —
but you are without and within.

Abba, remind me the essential is always unseen.

Do not fear those who can kill only your body.
After that you are safe; they can do no more.
Fear instead those who can buy your soul.
Have more respect than to value yourself too cheaply!
Who would give two cents for a couple of sparrows?
And yet our Father knows each one by name!
No need to fear. If God has his eye on a sparrow,
how far much more does his heart reach out to you?

If anyone stands for me in the face of the crowd,
the Son will stand for them in the presence of God.
But if anyone disowns me, fearing the jeers of the mob,
I will say before God, "I don't even know their names."
Those who reject me will be given another chance
to be forgiven, but who can save those who reject
the Spirit who forgives and their need to be forgiven?
When the faithless hem you round and taunt your faith,
be confident in God, for God is confident in you.
Be at peace! The Spirit will give you the words!

(Luke 12:4-12)

Hymn Dear secret greenness! nursed below
   Tempests and winds and winter nights!
Vex not, that but One sees thee grow;
   That One made all these lesser lights.

What needs a conscience calm and bright
   Within itself, an outward test?
Who breaks his glass, to take more light,
   Makes way for storms into his rest.

Then bless thy secret growth, nor catch
   At noise, but thrive unseen and dumb;
Keep clean, bear fruit, earn life, and watch
   Till the white-winged reapers come!

                      (Henry Vaughan)

Closing Holy Friend,
I hand over my soul to you
to be re-energized during the night
so I am ready to begin
again.
Amen.

158

Day Twenty-eight

Living God,   **Presence**
the sophisticated and the "cool,"
the defensive and the untrusting
miss so much of what life is for.
The crucifix gives them the lie.

Abba, arm me, like Jesus, with vulnerability.   **Grace**

As unthinkable as it might be for you to accept,   **Psalm**
you are God's Chosen People, the saints beloved by God.
Clothe yourselves, then, in sincere compassion;
let your armor be kindness, patience, humility, truth.
Bear with one another's weaknesses.
Forgive one another before the quarrel begins.
The Lord has forgiven you; now do the same.
Over all those clothes, to seal and certify them,
   put on love.
May the peace of Christ invade and subdue your soul.
It is for this we were called together
   as the Body of Christ.
Always be thankful. And always be channels of joy.
                                        (Colossians 3:12-17)

Shall I run and hide my fistful of stars?   **Hymn**
Or try to harvest them all?
Shall I sit inside, secure by the hearth
when the sky's on fire with their call?
Can a man abide the aching heart
to catch them up where they fall?
Just to sit and be makes a no one of me

159

when the gods make the wind blow fair.
    And it matters not if I find the spot.
    In the going, I'm already there.

When I stand and feel the wash of the rain
draw paths out over the sea,
then my heart goes stealing out to attain
horizons I've never seen.
Shall I turn my heel, a man in vain,
when gods are calling to me?
Oh, the call may lie, but until I die,
I must go when the wind blows fair.
    And it matters not if I find the spot.
    In the going, I'm already there.

Offering | God, my Friend,
this day is yours.
I offer you my acceptance
of whatever you send —
suffering, joy, toil, trouble —
ennobled far beyond my means
because it comes through the greatest gift
you gave me to offer,
Jesus, your Son, our Eucharist.
I pray not to change your mind,
only to understand it,
to yield to it.
But I do ask you to be with me,
especially in....
And I ask your loving watchfulness
for my friend....
Help me find you, through the day,
beneath all your surprising disguises.
Amen.

Living God,
moguls make millions convincing us
that nothing succeeds like
the appearance of success.
Remind me you look only
at my inside.

Presence

Abba, help me ignore what other people think.

Grace

God is my light and salvation. Whom should I fear?
Within his fortress, what can threaten me?
Even when everyone is against me — even myself —
I'd be a fool to fear when the Lord God calls me friend.
I ask only to live all my days in the house of God,
sheltered from all that seeks to ravage my soul.
No matter what comes, I will face it, head held high.
No matter my frailty, my God has chosen me.

(Psalm 27)

Psalm

Poor soul, the centre of my sinful earth,
These rebel powers that thee array,
Why dost thou pine within and suffer dearth,
Painting thy outward walls so costly gay?
Why so large cost, having so short a lease,
Dost thou upon thy fading mansion spend?
Shall worms, inheritors of this excess,
Eat up thy charge? Is this thy body's end?
Then, soul, live thou upon thy servant's loss,
And let that pine to aggravate thy store;
Buy terms divine in selling hours of dross;
Within be fed, without be rich no more;
So shalt thou feed on Death, that feeds on men,
And Death once dead, there's no more dying then.

(William Shakespeare)

Hymn

A soldier surrounded by enemies, if he is to cut his way out,
needs to combine a strong desire for living with a strange
carelessness about dying. He must not merely cling to life,
for then he will be a coward, and will not escape. He must

Reading

161

not merely wait for death, for then he will be a suicide, and
will not escape. He must seek his life in a spirit of furious
indifference to it; he must desire life like water and yet drink
death like wine.

(Gilbert K. Chesterton)

Scripture	Do not let your charity be just one more insincere mask. Hate only what is genuinely evil, and honor goodness wherever it shows itself true. Love one another as a good family does, and have profound respect for one another. Work hard without excuses and with open hearts and hands. If you hold on to hope, you will be honestly cheerful. Don't let go of that hope, even when trials come. Just keep on praying. If any of your fellow Christians are needy, share with them, and open your hearts to strangers.

(Romans 12:9-13)

Closing	God, my Friend, make me hypersensitive to what is not genuinely myself in me. Then help me uproot that. Amen.

EVENING

Presence	Living God, there must be some merit in imperfection, because you created us imperfect, and you knew what you were doing.
Grace	Abba, remind me that being fallible is okay.

Psalm	It is "comfortable" to sing God's praises;
	   so it must be right.
	There is a heady feeling, as if I know my proper place,
	on my knees at the knees of the Source
	   of stars and seas.

Such greatness, beyond calculation, humbles me.
And yet this Greatness stooped to embrace the wounded,
shared our toil, breathed our stink, knew death.
It is, as one king said, "a puzzlement."

The God who strewed the sable sky with stars,
the God who carved valleys with silver torrents,
the God who drew life from an ocean of molten rock,
the God who cracks the iron grip of ice
and sends the green juice that spurts into spring....
shared our toil, breathed our stink, knew death.
It is, as one king said, "a puzzlement."

(Psalm 147)

Achilles greets Odysseus in Hades:

Hymn

Do they still plant seeds in the springtime?
Do they still burn leaves in the fall?
And do colts still frisk when the air is brisk?
Are the pines on the hill still as tall?
Do old men in sunshiny doorways still tell lies
   and cackle and buzz?
And do autumn leaves still cling to your sleeves?
Is the world still as fine as it was?
Do the plains still ring with our battle cries?
Do the bards still sing of the wars?
Is there someone there who remembers my name?
Is the world still the same as it was?
Does the rain still shine on the rooftops?
Does it still smell sweet in the straw?
Is it still good to be a man, and free?
Is the word still as fine as it was?
Odysseus answers:
Yes, the seeds still fly in the autumn
and lie in the earth till spring.
And the leaves turn gold when the days get cold
and the cranes spread their red-golden wings.
Yes, the girls in frocks, white with sunset,
take their jugs to the stream at dusk,
and the old folks sigh for the days gone by.
Yes, the world's still as fine as it was.
There are some old men in their doorways

who still spin tales about us,
and they teach the boys the sound of your name.
Yes, the world's still the same as it was.
Still, the wind comes howling in winter
and sweeps on the fire with a rush.
But it's hard to care while the fire is there.
Yes, the world's still as fine as it was.

Closing | Holy Friend,
when my life seems inescapably grim,
remind me that unselfconscious laughter
is the only secret passage out.
Amen.

Day Twenty-nine

Living God,
there are really only two choices:
mumble and gripe in the dark
or go looking for some tinder.
So ignite my waterlogged soul.

Presence

Abba, give me some hope and I'll share it.

Grace

And you — you who believe you are only a child,
you are to be a prophet of the Most High God,
for you will go fearless before him to prepare his way.
You bring them good news: forgive and be forgiven!
You carry in your hands the tender mercy of God,
who will send his Son, the dawn of freedom, to us
to give hope to those enslaved to darkness and fear,
to light our way along the path to peace.

(Luke 1:76-79)

Psalm

Lord, let me be a torch that springs to light
    And lives its life in one exultant flame,
One leap of living fire against the night,
    Dropping to darkness even as it came.
For I have watched the smoldering of a soul
    Choked in the ashes that itself hath made,
Waiting the slow destruction of the whole,
    And turned from it, bewildered and afraid.
Light me with love — with hate — with all desire
    For that I may not reach, but let me burn
My little moment in pulsating fire
    Ere yet into the darkness I return;

Hymn

Be it for guard, or menace, peace or sword,
Make me thy torch to burn out swiftly, Lord.

(Theodosia Garrison)

Offering

God, my Friend,
this day is yours.
I offer you my acceptance
of whatever you send —
suffering, joy, toil, trouble —
ennobled far beyond my means
because it comes through the greatest gift
you gave me to offer,
Jesus, your Son, our Eucharist.
I pray not to change your mind,
only to understand it,
to yield to it.
But I do ask you to be with me,
especially in....
And I ask your loving watchfulness
for my friend....
Help me find you, through the day,
beneath all your surprising disguises.
Amen.

DAYTIME

Presence

Living God,
Doctor King said that
anyone who had nothing worth dying for
didn't deserve to live.
Then make me forge a life
worth dying for.

Grace

Abba, if time flies, then make me run.

Psalm

We are just the crockery that hold the treasure,
the drafty stables where God has chosen to dwell.
We, of ourselves, are not noble but ennobled;
our overwhelming power is not ours but God's.
But with God's power within us, we will prevail:
beset on all sides by troubles, but never cornered,

166

confused and perplexed, but never as far as despair,
surrounded by enemies but never without a Friend,
knocked down and battered, but never quite destroyed.
Wherever, whatever, we carry the Spirit of God;
in us the death and triumph of Jesus are bodied forth.
It is not ourselves we preach, but Jesus as Lord.
We face little deaths every day for the sake of Christ
so deaths can be turned to life as it was for him.

(2 Corinthians 4:7-12)

When I do count the clock that tells the time,
And see the brave day sunk in hideous night;
When I behold the violet past prime,
And sable curls all silver'd o'er with white,
When lofty trees I see barren of leaves,
Which erst from heat did canopy the herd,
And summer's green all girded up in sheaves,
Borne on the bier with white and bristly beard,
Then of thy beauty do I question make,
That thou among the wastes of time must go,
Since sweets and beauties do themselves forsake
And die as fast as they see others grow;
  And nothing 'gainst Time's scythe can make defence
  Save breed, to brave him when he takes thee hence.

(William Shakespeare)

The present life of men on earth, O king, as compared with the whole length of time which is unknowable to us, seems to me to be like this: as if, when you are sitting at dinner with your chiefs and ministers in wintertime…one of the sparrows from outside flew very quickly through the hall; as if it came in one door and soon went out through another. In that actual time it is indoors it is not touched by the winter's storm; but yet the tiny period of calm is over in a moment, and having come out of the winter it soon returns to the winter and slips out of your sight. Man's life appears to be more or less like this; and of what may follow it, or what preceded it, we are absolutely ignorant.

(Venerable Bede)

Scripture	We feel we must continually thank God for you, my friends. It's only right that we do, because your faith is growing so wonderfully, and the love you show for one another is deepening and spreading. Among all the communities, we take special pride in you — your faithful perseverance through all you've been forced to undergo. It shows how just God's judgment is, and your suffering now is an assurance that you are worthy of the kingdom of God. (2 Thessalonians 1:3-5)
Closing	God, my Friend, don't let me be afraid to wear myself out. When I'm finally called, it would be a pity if I had anything left unspent. Amen.

EVENING

Presence	Living God, like most people, I suppose, I'm uncomfortable making a fuss. But Jesus cleansing the Temple, bawling out the Pharisees, telling his first pope to get out of his sight — make me wonder if my reserve is always defensible.
Grace	Abba, don't ever let me say, "Oh, I'm nobody."
Psalm	You — no, don't look round! You are the salt of the earth. If the souls of those about you have any zest, let it be because of the tang you give to their lives. If the salt [if you] goes insipid, mediocre, stale, you are worse than merely useless to the rest of us.

You — no, don't look round!
  You are the only light in the room.
If the rest of us are pawing our way here in the dark,
then you have to shine! Show us the joy in your face!
If you hide that light (hide you) out of callow fear,
you smother the Light of the World and paralyze God.
                                        (Matthew 5:13-16)

It's really strange sometimes, don't you know,   **Hymn**
  That things go as well as they do.
When we think of the little — the very small mite —
  We add to the work of the few.
We sit, and stand round, and complain of what's done,
  And do very little but fuss.
Are we bearing our share of the burdens to bear?
  It isn't the church — it's us.

So, if want to have the kind of a church
  Like the kind of a church you like,
Put off your guile, and put on your best smile,
  And hike, my brother, just hike,
To the work in hand that has to be done —
  The work of saving a few.
It isn't the church that is wrong, my boy;
  It isn't the church — it's you.
                                        (anonymous)

Holy Friend,   **Closing**
I'm not quite up to a hike right now
or making a difference
or even complaining!
But I'd be grateful is we could
take that up again tomorrow.
Amen.

169

Day Thirty

Presence

Living God,
paradoxes, paradoxes!
Winners lose, losers win.
If you made our minds to find your will,
why didn't you build that in?
Fascinating.

Grace

Abba, be with me, going against the tide.

Psalm

Gifted are those with no grounds to be arrogant;
  the kingdom of God is their rightful inheritance.
Gifted are those whose hearts are still able to break;
  Christ who shared their sorrow will comfort them.
Gifted are those who are ready and willing to be used;
  those who cheerfully serve are truly in charge.
Gifted are those who submit to the will of God;
  God will fill them, full measure, brimming over.
Gifted are those possessed of forgiving hearts;
  certain it is that God will show mercy to them.
Gifted are those who refuse to be hypocrites;
  with their honest eyes they see the face of God.
Gifted are those who bring disputes to an end;
  they are the rightful sons and daughters of God.
Gifted are those who suffer for serving God;
  The kingdom of God is theirs, forever and more.
                            (Matthew 5:3-10)

Hymn

He borrow'd da bread when da crowd He fed
  On da grassy mountain side,
He borrow'd da dish of broken fish

With which He satisfied.
But da crown He wore and da cross he bore
  Was His own —
  Da cross was His own.

He borrow'd da ship in which to sit
  To teach da multitude;
He borrow'd a nest in which to res' —
  He had nebber a home so rude;
But da crown He wore an' da cross he bore
  Was his own —
  Da cross was His own.

He borrow'd a room on His way to da tomb
  Da Passover lamb to eat;
Dey borrow'd a cave for Him a grave,
  Dey borrow'd a windin' sheet.
But da crown He wore an' da cross he bore
  Was His own —
  Da cross was His own.

                                  (an unknown black poet)

Offering

God, my Friend,
this day is yours.
I offer you my acceptance
of whatever you send —
suffering, joy, toil, trouble —
ennobled far beyond my means
because it comes through the greatest gift
you gave me to offer,
Jesus, your Son, our Eucharist.
I pray not to change your mind,
only to understand it,
to yield to it.
But I do ask you to be with me,
especially in....
And I ask your loving watchfulness
for my friend....
Help me find you, through the day,
beneath all your surprising disguises.
Amen.

Presence	Living God, an Arab heart can live in a Jewish chest, a Black's kidney in a Klansman's back, a prostitute's corneas in a nun's eyes. What are these vacuous distinctions all about?
Grace	Abba, silence is shame.

Psalm	All round me, they whimper: "Run away! Hide! Quick!
	They have it in for you, you know.
	    They're in the shadows!
	Everything's falling apart! Why do you stand there?"
	
	I stand because the Lord God bids me to.
	His eye is on me, and I dare not turn away.
	But as he watches me, he also watches them,
	the world-beaters, the exploiters, the toadies,
	    the indifferent, the prim.
	God sends me to challenge them, fearlessly — not to win!
	Silence is shame. For me, the struggle is enough.
	I trust in God because God trusts in me.
	
	                      (Psalm 11)

Hymn	For Mercy has a human heart, Pity, a human face, And Love, the human form divine, And Peace, the human dress. Then every man, of every clime, That prays in his distress, Prays to the human form divine, Love, Mercy, Pity, Peace. And all must love the human form, In heathen, Turk, or Jew; Where Mercy, Love, and Pity dwell, There God is dwelling too. (William Blake)

He that can apprehend and consider vice with all her baits
and seeming pleasures, and yet abstain, and yet distinguish,
and yet prefer that which is truly better, he is the true wayfar-
ing Christian. I cannot praise a fugitive and cloistered virtue,
unexercised and unbreathed, that never sallies out and sees
her adversary, but slinks out of the race, where that immortal
garland is to be run for, not without dust and heat. Assuredly
we bring not innocence into the world, we bring impurity
much rather: that which purifies us is trial, and trial is by
what is contrary.

(John Milton)

Bless those who persecute you. Don't curse them; bless them! **Scripture**
Rejoice with those who have reason to rejoice; share
heartbreak with the heartbroken. Treat everyone you meet
with equal kindness. Never, never be condescending! Make
genuine friends with those who are poor. Don't allow yourself to become smug. Never repay a shrewd stab in the back
with a cleverer stab in the back. Bend over backward to live
in peace. Do not take vengeance out of God's hands. If those
who despise you are hungry, feed them. Ah! They're in-
capable of understanding kindness. You'll heap coals of fire
on their heads!

(Romans 12:14-21)

God, my Friend, **Closing**
I stand to be counted
because you bid me to.
Amen.

EVENING

Living God, **Presence**
you are unavoidable.
Oh, you know I've tried!
It's so stupid when I think
I can do it all by myself!

Abba, if you're with me, I can shout! **Grace**

Psalm	Let not the sorceress boast of her wisdom and skill. Let not the strong man strut and stride in his pride. Let not the victor vaunt his valor and verve. Let not the banker brag of her boldness and bluffs. Let not the sufferer moan, "No one suffers as I!" If you must boast, then boast only of this: the God who knows the roots and reasons for pain, the God who forgives even before I'm ashamed, the God who gave me freedom to foil his plans, the God who loves me more than I love myself — that one true God sees me and knows my name. <div align="right">(Jeremiah 9:22-23)</div>
Hymn	Father of all! in every age 　　In every clime adored, By saint, by savage, and by sage: 　　Jehovah, Jove, or Lord! Thou first great Cause, least understood, 　　Who all my sense confined To know but this, that thou art good 　　And I myself am blind.... What conscience dictates to be done, 　　Or warns me not to do, This, teach me more than hell to shun, 　　That, more than heaven to pursue. What blessings thy free bounty gives 　　Let me not cast away; For God is paid when man receives, 　　To enjoy is to obey. <div align="right">(Alexander Pope)</div>
Closing	Holy Friend, there is nothing profitable in dying, only in what comes before. Amen.

Also from Liguori Publications...